IMPRISONED BY PEACE

A VIEW APART

MATTHEW MAHER

Published by 55:11 Publishing LLC
1701 Walnut Street 7th Floor | Philadelphia, Pennsylvania 19103 USA
info@5511publishing.com | www.5511publishing.com

55:11 Publishing is committed to *Publishing with Purpose*. The company reflects
the philosophy established by the founders, based on Isaiah 55:11:
"So is My word that goes out from My mouth; it will not return to Me empty,
but will accomplish what I desire and achieve the purpose for which I sent it."

Book design copyright © 2017 by 5511 Publishing LLC. All rights reserved.
Cover design by Tim Janicki, Sight2Site Media, www.s2smedia.net

Published in the United States of America

ISBN: 978-0-9838517-9-0

Acknowledgements

FIRST AND FOREMOST, to my Lord and Savior Jesus Christ, whereas, apart from Him I can do nothing; and only Christ can make something out of the nothing that I am.

I gratefully acknowledge Mrs. Cherri Olsen for her poetically perfect and professional editing and writing skills. Mrs. Olsen, because of your godly wisdom and analytical precision, these contemplations have become pregnant with purpose to birth progression in the soul.

To my mother for her spiritual encouragement throughout this journey as well as keeping me grounded in the faith. Mom, you know your role and influence in this book, and honor is always yours.

To Pastor Victor Hudson for his pointed, passionate, and powerful deliverance of Christ, our bread, to the inmates at Mid-State Correctional Facility. Pastor Vic, thank you for showing me what real faith looks like in action. "I have work to do!" Your example in this dark place has been a perpetual light for me, and I will always thank our Father in Heaven for placing you here for ministry.

And to my fellow inmates who possess a skewed view. Thank you for presenting me with the opportunities to see with *A View Apart.*

I remain nothing, and ALL the glory, honor, and praise goes to God who has kept me Imprisoned by Peace, saying:

"And seek the peace of the city where
I have caused you to be carried away captive,
And pray to the Lord for it;
For in its peace you will have peace."
Jeremiah 29:7

Contents

IMPRISONED BY PEACE

Preface

I often ponder on evanescent thoughts and eternal contemplations that if uttered aloud may inspire others to consider me mad, but it is alleged that a crazy person does not practice self-examination and certainly never questions the state of his sanity. Therefore, I admit these contemplations defy reason, yet I insist they are true for they spring forth from the reality of my life in prison—and they explain the peace I experience in the midst of utter chaos and confusion.

I call my core convictions "a view apart"—a view far from the norm. Some of my observations and reactions are not logical, and they only make sense as I see Christ in all my circumstances. He is the one who controls my circumstances; hence, it is when I have my God-goggles ON that I see purpose and peace behind all things.

One *View Apart* is looking out the back, steel-barred window into the side yard of the prison. The area is closed in by two parallel stands of barbed wire fencing, with a dense forest of thick trees and brush auguring the impenetrability of the space beyond the fences. It is a view of presumed controlled chaos!

Some mornings, before the sun rises, the darkness outside the window would be complete if not for the prison's outside spotlights. I think about how light always comes through the darkness. The ground is covered with early morning dew that sparkles in the artificial lighting and contrasts with the glistening razors on the fences. I look out and know I am locked in, but I feel as though I am *Imprisoned by Peace*. I cannot understand this peace, but I know from Whom it comes.

People tend to perceive peace in a sunset, a stretch of beach bordered by a calm ocean or some similar sort of relaxed and quiet environment. I can say that peace isn't an image in perfect harmony, but rather an inner contentment that can be felt and seen in any setting. My peace is seen and felt through a steel-barred window, confined by razor-sharp fences, and secured by towers and armed guards. Through this, I perceive calmness and serenity, a paradigm of "Being Still" (Psalm 46:10). My peace, which is the peace of God, guards my heart and mind through Christ Jesus (Philippians 4:7).

Another *View Apart* is the rusted paint and woven steel of the locked gate that confines me. It is a presumed controlled restriction. I sit at the front table on the prison tier as I read, study, and contemplate such thoughts. From here, I watch as the traffic flows in and out of the tier at the discretion of our jailers. Most inmates desire nothing more than to get outside those locked gates; yet here I am, on the inside, thinking about the freedom that is already mine.

According to my jailers, I am locked up. So I wonder: Are you really locked up if you have no desire to get out? Yes, the guard locks the gate to keep inmates in; but if I do not want to escape the locked gate until it is opened for me, does this still mean I am confined? Of course I am confined. I am "locked up" by the world's standards, but I am "locked in" by God's standards and He says: "I give freedom to the prisoners" (Psalm 146:7). If I can confirm any truth in the Bible by my situation, I would testify that true liberty does not come by external circumstances.

My *View Apart* sees the gate as entrance and inclusion to peace, but confinement sees the gate as restriction and conclusion of freedom. In these next 40 contemplations, you will discern that liberty is the experience of the one who sees with the eyes of Christ, but imprisonment is the life of bondage for the one without Christ. We are only as free as we allow ourselves to be, and "where the Spirit of the Lord is, there is liberty" (II Corinthians 3:17).

This *View Apart* knows that being content makes a confined man free, and discontent makes a free man confined! So wherever you are when you read these thoughts—whether confined yet free or free yet confined—it is my hope and desire to challenge your view.

1. The Eyes of Faith

A day in confinement will be perceived differently through the lens of faith. My daily living conditions take place in a location ruled by chaos and tension, yet I possess a peace that exists inwardly—and is exhibited outwardly. Come in and join me as I share a routine day with you.

It is 5:35 A.M., and only two other inmates on our tier are awake. One is in the bathroom shaving, while the other is sketching. The artist appears to have never gone to sleep. Lights will shoot on in 20 minutes, which will awaken only a few more. Around 6:10 A.M., the Correction Officer's (CO) shouted command to "count up" will act as a free man's alarm clock—unfortunately, without the snooze button. The assigned CO may vary for the day, but it is usually the same housing officer for the long haul. An inmate knows how the day may go based on who is on duty, as some COs are stricter than others. We learn them, just as they attempt to learn us.

I have already done a core workout at the back of my tier, composed of various crunches and sit-ups, which comes out to about 500 different repetitions. I lay a sheet down on the concrete floor, and though my back meets the ground with every thrust of my torso, I know that I will only get out of the workout what I put into the workout. That's the physical!

The walk to the back of the tier alone is enough to work you out mentally, as the pre-light darkness is already a warm-up for what to expect in the day's activities. It's like walking to the back utility room of a basement, but I cannot allow this depressing sight to keep me from continually displaying light. That's the mental! So I keep my mind set on things above even when the things around me are trying to impede my vision.

Now I want to pray and go through my daily devotionals prior to the mess call for breakfast at 6:30. These words spoken and read—and not the mess-hall trays—provide the sustenance I need to get through the day. I am thankful for this morning "that I may cause NO MORE PAIN" (I Chronicles 4:9, 10; paraphrased). That's the spiritual!

I had to write this thought down from one of this morning's devotionals because I like it so much; it strengthens my outlook: "There is never a majestic mountain without a deep valley and there is never a birth without pain."[1]

It's 6:16; count-up came and went. Inmates are stirring, anxious for breakfast. The milieu is chaotic. I bring my focus back to reading. I cannot imagine enduring this environment through faithless eyes, where grub is the only reason to rise. At 6:30, "COUNT IS CLEAR" is announced over the public-address system; this means all inmates are present.

Now confinement at its finest begins, which is far from fine, but my eyes of faith see a lesson in every view. It's 8:10 A.M., and I have a job to go to in 20 minutes. I work as a teacher's assistant in the upstairs classroom. Many people think that work in prison is intended merely to pass the time, but I know I must not allow this precious time to go to waste.

At 11:30, lunch mess is called, and the tumultuous scene from the morning mess call is repeated: Several inmates are asleep and beginning to stir, while others rush noisily to the locked gate.

After lunch, I return to work, but at 1:20 I'm back on the unit. I got called down from work to pick up legal mail. Legal mail is a downer because it is often a reminder of the pain an inmate's actions caused. I choose to pray about my mail and release that which I have no control over. I refuse to dwell on negativity, and I whisper again: "That I may cause no more pain!" The distressing moment passes.

> **Tension ceases inwardly when you know WHO is with you through your storms.**

The choice is weathering the moments by His grace and strength as opposed to letting a storm brew for the day. Now it is time to write some letters. I am concerned about consistently replying to anyone who writes to me.

At 4:20 the dinner movement is fully engaged. The tier is clamorous, confusing, and discordant. No one is dozing. Two card games are going, the television is blasting, and the rest are conversing—but not so casually. Expletives fill the air and are an everyday, ever-present backdrop to the surroundings.

After the dinner mess, we have 5:30 recreation in the big yard. And that is exactly what it sounds like, it's just an open, big yard about the size of a 400-meter track—with loose weights scattered all throughout a designated area, a blacktop for basketball, and a patch of grass mixed with dirt for soccer. The big yard is an inmate's escape from the drudgery of the tier. I will get some exercise sets in, mixed with a montage of push-ups and pull-ups, depending on the night and the weather. My work-out in the yard changes nightly between cardio and weights, but it is always intense. The yard is chaos in motion, closed in by three 20-feet high, barbed-wire fences; the prison itself is the fourth "wall." Thirty-feet towers post up on each corner, with armed guards to watch for any aggressive activity. I usually just keep it moving and stay away from competition.

In prison, competition has no winner, for if you win, and the loser doesn't like this, he will make you lose—and I'm not talking about a rematch. Sometimes it is "compete at your own risk"—where the risk could be your life, your freedom or your future.

So I keep it moving! "Keep it moving" means to be socially active with every group. That is how I get to know everyone in here, and fortunately my outgoing personality has been like that my entire life.

It's 8:20 P.M.; rec was good and "safe." Now I am just observing the different activities on the unit. A fellow inmate grumbles to another, "This is such a waste of time, isn't it?" I think to myself, "No, *you* are wasting your time." For many, prison is just a timewaster—with no purpose, no substance, no productivity, no peace.

At 11 P.M. I am still awake, and this is unusual. Lights are out, the TV set is off, but the turbulent cacophony continues unabated and seems even magnified, draped in the dark of the night.

My *View Apart* through the eyes of faith overrides the external conditions. Confined, but set free. I thank God that I'm *Imprisoned by Peace*.

2. Moments, Yes, but Not Often

On the phone one night, my brother Anthony asked me a question that many are reluctant to ask, yet many insist on answering for me based on what the world thinks. He said, "Do you ever get discouraged in there, and are you shocked to be in prison?" I replied, "Moments, yes, but not often. And I am shocked every time I look around at this dark environment, but I am at peace. The discouragement and shock are moments that I do not let get in the way of God's plan and purpose for this storm."

It's sad that when we speak of prison or the "storms" of life, we usually define the state of mind and spirit by the tempest that arises in that storm, and rightfully so, considering human nature. But what is faith *for* then? Now, there is nothing wrong with the questions asked, but I find a problem in the presumed answers.

If I were to take on the presumed answer of that question, which would involve perishing under the waves of my circumstances, then I would have no faith and everything is for nothing. I believe there is a reason for every confinement (mental or physical), and a reason for every "storm" in life.

> **I think we forget that Christ is with us in our storms, the very storms that He commands and calms.**

Still, we become startled when they hit us. I am living the truth that all that is required to sustain us through a storm is to rely on God. Faith allows me to answer, "Moments, yes, but not often."

I guess I did not mind my brother's question because it came out of concern; but when questions like that arise, I always wonder what it must be like for my family to answer others' questions about me. People may say to my parents, "How is your youngest?" Or they may ask my brothers, "What's Matt doing these days?" We can all imagine the presumptions that fill the minds of those inquisitive individuals when my family members lurch haltingly through the answer: "Oh, um, he is in prison."

Yes, I am in prison; but in a crazy way, I and my family are thankful that we are presented with these questions, because without the questions there can be no answer of "moments, yes, but not often" and the follow up of "because Christ sustains in the midst of storms, in the middle of chaos, and through any confinement." It is an oxymoron to have "thankful" and "imprisoned" refer to the same person in the same sentence, but, similarly, bitter is often combined with sweet—bittersweet! It's a rainbow after the rain, a diamond in the rough.

"Do you ever get discouraged in prison, and are you ever shocked to be in prison?"

"Moments, yes, but not often," as I desire to show how God has transformed me for the better—in prison. I want to show how God has saved my life—through this prison. "Moments, yes, but not often," as it is important to me that people know God is in complete control at all times—and that prison doesn't define me, nor does it have to confine me, but it can refine me.

I am at peace in this prison because my *View Apart* does not respect discouragement, and the shock is what keeps me active. All in all, I would rather be asked if I am afraid or discouraged or shocked, than to have Jesus ask me as He asked others, "Why are you fearful, O you of little faith?" (Matthew 8:26). With all glory, praise, and thanksgiving to God, I say, "My faith sustains."

3. Whatever the Weather

Whatever the weather on the outside, for an inmate, it is likely to affect the inside. From scorching summer days to the biting cold, from clear skies to cascading precipitation, in this bird cage where I reside it is blatantly obvious how the weather affects an inmate's morale.

An inmate is more likely to quiet down on a rainy day, and that is dangerous as many of an inmate's behaviors are naturally predisposed to boredom. Our minds are left wandering, leaving expressions of despair on our faces. These expressions have forced me to consider the tendencies that weather promotes—fostering the comprehension that whatever the weather, we must weather the weather.

Consider the importance of rain for an inmate. Because the outside is dreary, we focus all of our attention on the inside, where there is nothing to look at except drab walls and a restless environment. What do we allow our minds to conjure during these times? Our minds are left tested by our surroundings.

I appreciate the introspection and slower pace induced by the rain, because this weather situation reinforces my mindset which is fortified by faith. Likewise in life's afflictions, when that "gloomy rain" comes and causes bewilderment and a sense of hopelessness, believers can look within themselves for the power to "Be Still." Spiritually speaking, when your inside is calm, it does not matter how much outside turmoil "rains down" or "heats up." "You are of God . . . and have overcome . . . because greater is He that is in you, than he that is in the world" (I John 4:4). Prison gives me the time to live this reality. When our circumstances on the outside are screaming at us and threatening to defeat us, it is important that we look inside to quiet the storm.

When the day is beautiful—with clear blue skies, a warm sun, and a gentle breeze—it is easy to zone out in a good way. In the prison yard, I find myself focusing on the few white clouds instead of the 20-feet-high barbed wire fences and the even taller guard towers. The activity all around the prison yard is noisy and disorderly, but a well-meaning attempt at organization—with 18 or more playing soccer on a 50-yard dirt field with broken goals, while others engage in a full-court basketball game on a sand-patched blacktop with bent rims, and numerous inmates are scattered across the weight pit where they are working out or simply hanging out.

If the weather is bright and shiny and comfortable, we are more inclined to feel cheerful and to reflect the fair weather (and good times) in a pleasant personality. The opposite is equally true: When the weather (and life) becomes tempestuous, we reflect the disturbing circumstances by becoming stressed and negative. This should not be the case, as whatever the weather, we should weather the weather. So why does the "bad" in life have to bring out the worst in us? And can we in fact be different than what our surroundings are speaking to us?

My *View Apart* remains consistent in sun or rain, because I know that the true Son reigns!

Whatever the weather in life, I know that the peace of God may be seen, felt, and possessed. Whether it is a major tragedy or a minor difficulty, what we ultimately focus on during that weather makes all the difference.

> **We can magnify the circumstance or magnify God in our circumstance.**

I do not bring anything to the table that my neighbor doesn't bring with life experiences, but I have made a choice to lay my burden down at God's feet—as opposed to laying down in defeat.

I see the effects of weather here daily, combined with the mental and physical effects of confinement in a chaotic environment; and although I am in the rain, I have my umbrella of Peace. We must trust in the Son who reigns to control our surroundings, rather than allow our surroundings of sun or rain to control us. Only then will our outside turmoil be the means by which our inside gets calm.

4. The Gate

One thing about prison is that when they lock the gate, we are locked in, and there is nothing we can do about it. I hear our tier-block gate shut, "SLAM!"; and every time it closes, I'm still not used to the sound, but I'm now used to the reason behind the *locked gate.*

When you first arrive in prison, this unnatural state of captivity takes some getting used to. Every movement is reliant on a CO's discretion as to whether or not the gate should be opened for the task at hand.

As inmates, closed and locked gates are the norm, and we must not question the reasons behind it. I am no longer fazed by the sight of the locked gate, because I know that when it is unlocked, then I will walk through it. Until then I wait patiently.

Likewise in life, we are always looking for that open door hoping for that one opportunity, but when it shuts on us, "SLAM!" we get discouraged and begin to question God. We never come to the understanding that these closed doors and locked gates are a God-send.

We say in prison, "It is what it is"; and sometimes a "closed way" brings us closer to the right way.

> **What appears to be a dead end is in fact a direction to turn around and go the other way; there is always a reason behind a closed door.**

"SLAM!" Do not lose faith when a door closes: "See I have set before you an open door and no one can shut it. For you have a little strength, have kept My word and not denied My name" (Revelation 3:7).

An inmate knows he is powerless, and it is confirmed by the sound and authority of the gates opening and closing. He is at the mercy of the corrections officers on duty, they control who or what goes in and out. It is the gatekeepers who are responsible for the prison's integrity and as I witness the significance of the opening and closing of the gate, I realize there is much power and control in the hands of those who possess the gate.

In ancient cities, protection of the front gate was the most important foundation to maintaining a secure city. Essentially, whoever "possessed the gate" controlled the city's integrity and power. But, as time went on, the cities' enemies realized that in order to breach the city, all they had to do was to enter the front gate by way of bribery. Those who held the power of the city in their hands and "possessed the gate" could eventually succumb to the enemy's tricks, and the integrity of the city could be compromised.

It is easy to falter with that much control and power. Who or what we allow to occupy those gates can mean the difference between what is a *hard breach* or a *breathe easy*, for the city finds its rest based upon its safety.

Although as an inmate, I cannot control the gate, I still have the ability to possess the most important gate—the gate to my heart. Who or what we allow into our hearts reflects the integrity of our being. When we allow Jesus to "possess our gate," He in return allows us to enter His.

"Unless the Lord builds the house, they labor in vain who build it; unless the Lord guards the city, the watchman stays awake in vain" (Psalm 127:1).

It is under His possession that we may breathe easy, but we must always be prepared for the hard breach, for our enemy wants nothing more than to "possess the gates" of our hearts. So as we open our hearts and allow Jesus to occupy that gate, He declares that He Himself is now the gate of the door.

"I am the door! If anyone enters by Me, he will be saved" (John 10:9).

It is at that point that we may confidently "enter His gates with thanksgiving and into His courts with praise" (Psalm 100:4). To "possess the gate" is to control the peace of the city, and it is with our hearts that we choose to either believe or be deceived.

The sight and sound of the gate in prison! "SLAM!" But my *View Apart* sees Jesus as the gate, and with it He may do as He pleases. Therefore, being hinged into Him assures me that a closed gate is a protected heart, and an open gate is where His possession starts!

The Gate, opened or closed? It matters not, for it is His.

5. Forget or For God?

I do not desire to forget, I desire for God. Had I not gone through tragedy, by my own doing, I would not be where I am today: incarcerated but liberated. I would take back only one thing from my past, and that is the life that was taken due to my irresponsible decision to drink and drive—all else would remain. But even a life lost has been the means necessary for my pain that deeply motivates me.

> We cannot take things back, but we can choose on how we look back.

One of the common beliefs of an inmate is upon one's release to never look back. "Forget this place and the reason you are here," many exclaim. Nobody wants to be here longer than they have to, but I have come to view my prison as peace and my tragedy as treasure. I will not forget, for God has allowed me to pass through both in order to save my life. I will not forget what motivates me, for God is behind everything that happens in life—both trials and triumphs.

I look back now with perfect hindsight, and I realize this encasement of God's grace would not allow my situation to just be a bad happening for me, but it was God's best plan for me. That's the difference between being imprisoned and *Imprisoned by Peace.*

Therefore, I will not forget this place or what I have done—not to dwell on them, but to use them for what God wants done. As A.W. Tozer once said, "It is doubtful whether God can use a man greatly until He hurts him deeply."[1] Consequently, I was plagued with sorrow and doubt prior to this confined peace, but deep down inside I knew that God had an ultimate plan for me; thus, I do not desire to forget, but I desire for God!

Now I know that I had to be broken deeply in order to be used greatly. For God has chosen me in spite of my sin and in spite of this place, and that is why I will not forget! I am right where I need to be, and this is God's best plan for me. I cannot forget a single thing of my ugliness, for God uses everything to make beauty.

Forget the pain? Nope. Forget the family? Nope. Forget the path? Nope. Forget the environment? Nope. Forget the ignorance? Nope. Forget this place and what I have done? Nope, for God knows I am deserving of only one thing: to be right where He wants me to be.

"For God works all things together for good"(Romans 8:28)—even our ugly past!

I am certainly ashamed for what I have done, but God uses our shame to glorify His name. I will forget the common belief to FORGET, because though I may not have chosen this plan and path for myself, it is FOR GOD to use as He pleases. I must always remember and while many may not see it this way, this is my *View Apart* for God knows the issues of my heart.

6. Breaking Boredom

Analyzation without self-examination makes condemnation. I view my environment with an open eye, a curious brow, and an eager heart. I see things daily that others see, but I choose to view them differently from most. In an environment that is set in its ways on so many levels, it is very rare to go against the grain; but going against this grain is a crop worth picking. I know very well how persuasive the boredom of this place can be, and I have watched as so many have given up in this monotonous battle, surrendering to "it" day after day.

Many view this boredom or "dead time" as inactivity or simply being tired; but one must distinguish the difference between being tired or bored. They don't see boredom taking the form of an all-day nap, vegetating in front of the TV, or a 24-hour pinochle card game. Boredom is a state of mind; and when our mind is left unstimulated, we convince ourselves we are tired. Now, I am in no position to judge anyone's heart and mind, but from my point of view, the "dead time" spent by inmates is exactly that, *dead*. It is clearly evident that how an inmate uses his time in the present will impact the future.

When we fail to use this "dead time" alive and active, we allow boredom to break down our minds and spirits and even our bodies. We make room for boredom and give it excuses to harbor in our lives; and even when "it" creeps into a relationship, we believe it is incompatibility.

Boredom will convince you to find pleasure in dark places.

This numb state of mind will cause you to settle into a complacent lifestyle, where nothing seems to arouse energy or emotion. And even with movement of everyday life, activity is not productivity. I know that I am in prison; and we are confined here, but our minds do not have to be.

> **It does not matter where we may find ourselves in life, when we are faced with a choice on how to spend our time, our decisions reveal the priorities of the heart.**

We may be locked up in body, but we do not have to be locked up in heart, mind, and spirit.

Dead time does not have to be dead.

I see boredom and the hold it has on my fellow inmates' minds daily. It's really the nature of this place, so after contemplating about "dead time" and being bored, I have tried to avert the negative affects it can have on me by embracing parts of boredom as a friend rather than a foe.

For example, I believe I am learning the tricks that Boredom can play on dulling my mind. He is subtle and cunning and requests an invitation to all alike. So I say, "Come on in, Boredom"; and when I have him where I want him, I am able to reverse his proposal.

He says, "Go lie down and do nothing, you deserve it. I will do your thinking!" So I oblige and proceed to my bed to lie; but without his direction, I begin to pray: "Meditate within your heart on your bed, and be still" (Psalm 4:4).

He then says, "Go watch some TV and stimulate your mind!" So I learn that for Boredom, it's not about the behavior the TV promotes, but the productive behavior the TV prevents. And I am motivated even more to tune the TV out.

Finally he says, "Look at your surroundings. Don't they have what you want? They relax all day and sleep as they please." So I consider my ways and realize that Boredom has taught me plenty today, and I am thankful for this lesson. My *View Apart* is breaking boredom and not allowing boredom to break me. I am going to continue to keep my eye on Boredom, knowing that it is better for him to have my eye than to have my mind.

7. More Noise in Our Silence

There is much more to silence than meets the ear. I am around noise all day and all night living on a tier with 38 men. Constant chatter, nonstop commotion, perpetual disturbance. So silence is a sweet and welcome respite; but it is tender, delicate, and fragile. And if misused by our thoughts, it can quickly become noise.

Late one night, with silence at last blanketing the darkness, an excruciating sound suddenly broke through with no warning. Confused and anxious, we jumped up to decipher the reason behind the noise. What we discovered was one of our fellow inmates, with no respect for the silence or regard for the rest of us, dragging the heavy metal table on the tier to his area. The sound of the metal legs screeching at stratospheric decibels as they were forced across the concrete floor created a din that was responsible for inciting a stampede of elephants inhabiting the savannah grasslands of Africa. The uproar continued and grew, as many inmates became enraged.

I sat up in my bed and watched as the perpetrator gave the perfect response to his clamorous transgression—an answer that confirmed the devil's plot to drown out the silent voice of

God with chaos, noise, and commotion. The perp said pridefully, "This is ####### prison. Go back to sleep!"

This ill-mannered reply was met with even more rude rebuttals, thus silence was removed completely from the remedy. I sat there in amazement as I realized that the populace often creates noise to distract, intimidate or gain attention for the noisemaker. Sometimes, our response to the noise merely adds to the present tumult. Now I am fully convinced there must be much more to silence if the world fears its entrance. Silence rarely has its way in here; but if it does and when it does, I know I must be ready to use it. "Be silent in the presence of the Lord God" (Zephaniah 1:7).

My *View Apart* has taught me that silence creates an atmosphere for clear listening, free observance, and stilled anxiety.

> Silence allows our hearts and minds to think, and our spirit to feel God's peace.

Now it makes total sense why the world desires to block this out. In silence, we may experience the "noise" of blessing and comfort. With our own attempts to break through the world's commotion and with our own accusations, our voice only adds to the tyranny of noise. Thus, we miss the marvel that would follow in our silent response, for we must follow the example of Jesus himself, who made them marvel greatly in His silence. "Then Pilate said to Him, 'Do You not hear how many things they testify against You?' But He answered Him not one word, so that the governor marveled greatly" (Matthew 27: 13, 14). "And when oppressed and afflicted, Jesus opened not His mouth" (Isaiah 53:7).

If I can catch this silence in a place of unceasing noise, and learn to prepare in that silence, then maybe I will be able to make more noise for God's glory. But silence in prison is always interrupted, and done so abruptly. Thoughts are broken and preparation thwarted. An attempt to make it right only adds to the wrong. This is why I am convinced of the power of silence; and if I can just grasp it while it remains, even in suffering, I will not speak out foolishly.

Likewise, as with an approaching storm, calm is always prior to the noise; and it is during this time of silence that one must prepare. Essentially, preparation opens us to the entry of peace when the chaos arrives, for it is impossible to be immobilized by a storm when you are centralized in Christ. Therefore, whether before the storm, in the storm or after the storm, "there is a great calm" with Jesus (Matthew 8:26).

8. Better Than the Beginning

As time goes on, it is difficult for an inmate to tell if he is progressing. Just because the time goes, it does not mean that progress goes with it. In life, we often equate the natural movement of time with advancement, but as I witness in here on a daily basis, time served does not mean that one served his time well.

Recently, one of my fellow inmates was released after serving six years in prison. I have only known him for the past six months, which is a lot of time of interaction in here, but his mind progression did not line up with his "time in" progression. Understandably, he became more enthusiastic as his release date approached, and it became extremely evident that "the end of a thing is better than the beginning" (Ecclesiastes 7:8).

But are we better off in mind, body, and spirit now than we were in the beginning?

When you are just starting out, whether it is a business project, a fitness program, or—yes—even a prison sentence, you would hope that finishing it would be a good feeling: a sense of accomplishment. You never want to be where you were when you started because the progression from beginning to end should be easily noted. There should be a change in the positive direction, and it should be obvious.

But how can an inmate measure his progress?

An inmate can stare at the clock and the calendar for as long as he wants, but this movement of time does not automatically set one's mind, body, and spirit toward improvement. Usually, starting out on any new journey is tough; and certainly one would expect to be initially miserable when coming into an environment like prison. But after several months or years, shouldn't that misery wear off? Of course it is only natural to become excited as the conclusion approaches, but what mindset are we taking with us at the end? One that has matured with the time or one that has ignored the opportunity that comes with time?

As time continues to go, so must our progression show! I wonder: Am I progressing the way I am supposed to? Will my end be better than my beginning? Constant interaction with the same individuals makes it hard to gauge if I am moving in a positive direction with the time. I have gotten used to my tier mates' behaviors, and they have probably gotten used to mine. Stagnation or negative progress, such as bitterness, is the condition of many through imprisonment. Many look back and are frozen or they look ahead and are frightened. It doesn't have to be that way!

> **My *View Apart* is that the past is forgiven and gone, the present is supplied with power for progression, and the future is bright with hope.**

Therefore, I have learned that the measure of our progress is in the fruit we bear and the light we reflect—not in the time that passes!

In a dark environment, a light should show forth no matter what—even a small candle can illuminate an entire room. However, in doing so, IT CONSUMES ITSELF, which is the desired end for the one who seeks to serve God while serving time—knowing that SELFishness cannot exist within for Christ to truly shine without. Even Jesus told us a similar truth: "For whoever desires to save his life will lose it, but whoever loses his life for My sake will find it" (Matthew 16:25).

Yet, have I consumed myself by my spiritual and mental progression at this point? Have I found life by the way I've served this time (which is about serving and not always thinking of mySELF)? The men in here act as if time served is lost time, and they will never get it back. They are exactly right. We will never get any time back, so redeem the time by moving forward in mind, in body, and in spirit. Not only should the end of a thing be better than the beginning, but let us achieve positive progress along the way.

9. Popular Opinion

Talk about me, I don't mind. Hate me, no worries. Despise what I've done, I do too. Offer your "Popular Opinion," why not? Give your support, much appreciated. Condemn the message, why would you? I should not have a platform, did not ask for one. Quench my voice, then you speak up? Understand the pain, I doubt you do. Feel sorry for me, no thanks. Empathy, not even that.

I made a mess, no doubt. Now you want me to walk away from this mess, doubt that. Help clean, your choice. Ignore, no problem. Hate the mess, not the message. It's my fault, I know this too. Any good done, it's not me anyway. I will claim my bad, but must pass on the good. I am not my own (I Corinthians 6:19) and was bought with a price (v. 20). The good is God. The bad is mine. Forgiven, I am. Humbled, for sure. Complaints, none. Content, learned. Peace, imprisoned by it.

> **I may have done what they said I've done, but I do not have to listen to who they say I am.**

I am me, a sinner saved by grace. I only have one voice, and you can't take that from me. Hate the man, not the message. You're entitled!

Yet I still ponder poetically . . .
Am I to write what people expect to hear?
Or do I write the truth of what I think and feel?
I choose feelings and convictions over popular opinion,
And the strongly acceptable idea of "what is prison."
So I must thank God for how far He's allowed me to
    come,
Because before this journey began, my mind was straight
    numb.
I still have no excuses or complaints,
And I praise the Lord for removing all restraints.
For I have never been more at peace, with determination,
Regardless of what popular opinion says of incarceration.
"It is what it is"—my complete submission to His will;
That and prayer, and then devotion to "Be Still."
I can contemplate, "Woe is me, and I just can't go on";
But that's a lie, and I can't picture myself singing that
    song.
So I march to the beat of a different drum—
One that was modeled by God's only begotten Son.
Although I awake and it's prison bars that I see,
Therefore, I pray and I pray, "Lord God, go before me."
Then BOOM! A slam of the prison gate;

Back to reality and reminded again of the poor decision
    I made.

Right then the devil is presented his opportune time,

But it's too late 'cause I live by the message of this rhyme.

And this is directed to the popular opinion:

My life, this prison, my future: God's dominion!

This is my core conviction and the imprisonment of
    peace that I feel,

Contemplations so raw and a *View Apart* so real!

10. Inner Battle

To be stuck in prison with some of the most crude and vulgar people is unbearable at times. I see the constant display of disrespectful actions, deliberately intended to empty others of their joy. Where there is no respect, there is no mutual agreement; with no agreement, there is no harmony; and the absence of harmony equals chaos. This ignorant behavior would steal my peace, if my hold on it were not tightly gripped. So I attempt to remove myself from the chaos, but where does one go in a state of confinement?

When the overwhelming majority is controlled by ignorance, how can one counter that? Has my peace reached its limits? As a light in the darkness, I desire to divide the darkness. But from this view, ignorance seems to be doing all of the dividing, and the devastation I feel in my soul is tragic.

"If anyone is ignorant, let him be ignorant" (1 Corinthians 14:38). The context of this Scripture refers to ignorance as a condition of choice.

So what is the remedy? I can only let so much disrespect go on before it *must* be addressed, but then I become the bad guy. I may speak up for what's right, when a silent example is not enough, but then they look at me as if I am the problem. So do I allow the wrongful behavior to go on or do I bring the ignorance to light?

Welcome to the ultimate mental struggle in prison! Herein lies the battle: to do right all the time, even when doing right is perceived as wrong because it violates the cultural code. When you are seen as wrong, everything you do is then evaluated, misinterpreted, and judged. You may be different, but it is that very difference that is despised by the ignorant.

Sight can sometimes be a menace to my true vision, my *View Apart*. Seeing the ignorance in here sometimes blinds the light by which I live, and hearing the ignorant can smother my peace by provoking enmity and negativity. Once again, what we allow into our minds will eventually find its way out. I have no room for such division anymore, and I only desire to add to my environment harmony with agreement and subtract from the surrounding chaos with peace. This inner battle is a war worth fighting, for without it there would be no contemplations.

These contemplations (my inner thoughts) are intended, honorably and purely, for increasing my understanding of God and spiritual things—that I may grow ever closer to Him. The devil hates spiritual growth, and that is why Jesus often spoke of seeds and the fruit they produced in the course of "growth." As recorded in the Bible, we will know believers by the "fruit" that they bear; so if other people or situations can choke such growth, there will be no difference between a dead weed and a healthy seed. And there must be an obvious difference!

"The fruit of the Spirit is: love, joy, peace, longsuffering, kindness, goodness, faithfulness, gentleness, self-control" (Galatians 5:22). These fruits will show out when we water them within.

The remedy to the struggle and the resolution to the inner battle: to do right ALL the time; ignore the ignorance; and let your light so shine before men (Matthew 5:16). I know where I am and the ignorance that exists here, but this environment cannot hurt me unless I allow it.

> I was built for these tests, and by these tests I am able to build character. I am thankful for these inner battles and for the growth thereafter.

As John Bunyan said, "If my life is fruitless, it doesn't matter who praises me, and if my life is fruitful, it doesn't matter who criticizes me."

11. What's Good?

As the PA system announced, "Unit 7, Rec in the Big Yard," my thoughts were reflecting on the question, "What's good?" When I got out into the yard, I proceeded to the farthest corner, where old wooden benches outline what once was a baseball diamond. I decided to lie down on my back on one of those benches for the entire two-hour rec period. As I stretched out on the bench with my face up, the blinding summer sun forced my eyes shut; and I was able to contemplate deeper on "what's good?" This question has been on my mind since I came across it in Micah 6:8: "He has shown you, O man, what is good."

Yep, just when you thought the greeting "what's good" was a new way to say "what's up" or "how are you," the prophet Micah coined this saying from the Lord thousands of years ago. I thought about how very common it is for a conversation between inmates to open up with "What's good?" I wondered if they really knew what they were asking with this phrase. Then I opened my eyes as a cloud covered the sun's rays, and the air became momentarily chilled. Still I enjoyed my comfortable position, reclining on my back, facing the sapphire sky, milk-white clouds, and radiant sun.

Instantly, my attention went to the fact that when my neck remained straight, eyes upward, the true view above was open and "good." Then, when I turned my neck to the right or left, the true view changed drastically, becoming closed and confined by barbed wire fences; but it was still "good" in my sight.

As the cloud moved away from the sun, my eyes were forced shut again, and new thoughts surfaced in my mind.

> My heart smiled as I said in my head, "You can be free and confined in your circumstances or you can be confined and free in your circumstances."

But how can such freedom through such confinement be good? A larger cloud now obstructed the sun, and I opened my eyes to this prison, this big yard, the fortified boundaries and high towers; and I realized that no matter which way my neck directed my sight, it was still good because God is always good. I have found that if I do what the Lord has shown me and requires of me, no matter where I am, then that is "what's good." I sat up to adjust my shorts and then lay back down again on the rugged wooden bench, closed my eyes this time willingly, and began to pray.

"What's good, Lord?"

"Simple, My son: Do justly, love mercy, and walk humbly with Me."

My *View Apart* agrees, "Now, that's good!" And the PA system bellowed, "Rec in the Big Yard is terminated!"

12. In'Car'ceration

I frequently look back on this journey and find great value and lessons in review.

I ask God, "Who am I that You have taken me this far?" I find myself in awe of the curves we navigated, the bridges we crossed, and the tunnels we passed through—having arrived to this day safe and secure, and all in the appropriate timing and necessary mileage. This retrospective drive down "memory lane" is worth taking, as I am able to see how far I have come mentally, physically, and spiritually; and I am excited to go farther. I ask God another question: "Where are we going, Lord?"

I am able to answer my own question with the words of Ezekiel (37:3): "O Lord God, You know." I must simply follow along and trust the one who already knows where we are going. Like a child who is able to fall asleep in the backseat of his father's car, certain that when he awakes his father will have brought him safely to their destination, I too *rest* as my Father in Heaven drives this in'CAR'ceration. (NOTE: The Hebrew meaning for *rest* is "to be at peace.")

Occasionally, when I glance out the side-view mirror on this drive, I am quickly reminded that "objects in the mirror are closer than they appear." Not willing to be distracted or deceived by that view, which is my past, I shift my attention back to the front, which is the future. ALL that I have passed on this drive is my past, and it is behind me. But I must check the rearview mirror periodically to see how far I have come and to avoid the troubles that exist there by proper preparation for the next passage. I do that, no longer encumbered by worries or fears because it is my Father who is safely driving this in'CAR'ceration!

At this very moment, I look around and see so many attempting to drive their own in'CAR'cerations; and I cannot help but be saddened by the roads traveled with no direction. It was a crash-and-burn that warranted all of us here today, but even during this time of repair for the damage done, many choose to continue on with no map, no gas, and no clear vision. Some are stuck in the rear view, missing everything in front of them, while others are only concerned with speeding ahead. With no guidance or plan, their trips will once again be a fall.

But this was once me too, as I attempted to drive myself on numerous occasions. I fought for the wheel, and God allowed me to travel often the hard way. I never realized until now that each and every stop along the way was necessary for me to learn to finally be a passenger on this journey. I thought I was leading, yet I was a hitch-hiker all along—stranded without a ride and settling for anyone who would pull over to pick me up.

I **park**ed myself in prison because I got into the wrong CAR—and drove it while intoxicated by my own doing; but now sober-minded and surrendered, I am finally allowing God to **drive** this in'CAR'ceration. It is a forward trek of inestimable value that I may never **reverse** backward to my old ways, nor again be **neutral** to my faith but steadfastly maintain my internal timing at "Be Still."

"Are we there yet, Father?" I ask, and I hear the biblical response again: "O Lord God, You know!" Amen.

13. Opened For View

I have seen some devious actions go down here in the past few years. Intentions and behaviors that I was never around for the first 25 years of my life; so, needless to say, I had to learn quickly how to tell the difference between a well-intended inmate and the ill-intended one. Some would take the shirt right off your back, and then look at you strangely when you asked for your shirt back. Others will use your kindness until it runs dry, leaving you wet behind the ears to what just happened. Prison is not a place to play with, but then again it is not a place that I had ever figured I'd be living.

It was difficult to find a telling behavior that would pinpoint whether the intentions of my fellow inmates were for good or for bad. There have been plenty of times when I thought someone was ill-willed, and it turned out not to be the case. How could I discern the difference?

So I watched and studied their conduct and comportment as if they were test subjects, but still to no avail. Sometimes I was dead on and sometimes dead wrong. There had to be an easy way to figure this out. Was there another view? What was I missing? Then I found the answer as clear as day (light); and regardless of the manipulation (fog), and even those who hid their intentions by night (dark), I could finally see the difference without having to see any behaviors or tendencies. No more guessing. No more waiting for an outcome. No more lessons learned through harsh experience.

The answer was staring right at me all along, and the only chance for anyone to conceal the truth was to put a lid on it. An *eyelid* that is! "The lamp of the body is the eye. If therefore your eye is good, your whole body will be full of light. But if your eye is bad, your whole body will be full of darkness" (Matthew 6: 22-23). Now I see it!

Darkness. Lightness. And even shadowy gray.

Some try to hide their gaze, knowing that the "eyes are the windows to the soul." But you cannot conceal or disguise what is open; and when *opened for view*, what comes out? Some eyes are fierce, hostile, and hard. Some eyes contain no joy and have lost the twinkle that shows interest or sympathy.

> **What their eyes choose to view is what dwells on the mind.**

Thus, we are what we see—as our eyes reveal our feelings, without the necessity for actions or words. It's the difference between compassion and callousness, forgiveness and resentment, good and evil, and ultimately light and darkness. I can't read minds, but I can now read eyes, which—sooner or later—are always opened for view.

Choosing the absence of light is choosing not to see—or be seen. I once saw an inmate try to disguise his darkness by wearing shaded glasses, but "the lamp of his body, the eye" began to argue and complain with its owner—it couldn't see, not even to perform its own deviousness! My *View Apart* must be able to find humor in such ill-will, for then I am able to find heavenly peace in an earthly hell.

14. Come Back to Yourself

Where have I been most of my young life thus far? I have been all over the country in my travels with soccer, from childhood as a novice player to adulthood as a professional athlete. I have been to so many great colleges and universities, visiting those campuses either for pleasure or sports-related activities. I have even lived in some beautiful cities in my day. But where have I been while being where I was? Now in prison, I realize that though I have been all over and claimed to be a man of faith, I made this claim when I was "beside myself." I never fully understood that I was going through the motions in life spiritually and that there needed to be a catalyst that would bring me "back to myself." I found my way from here to there, but I was lost!

This *View Apart* from my prison experience is not about "finding God in jail," as so many say. Unfortunately, nobody "finds" God, for *He* was never hiding. That cliché of "finding God in prison" comes from the blunt reality that a prisoner has no one to turn to behind these walls, and it is in these desperate times of loneliness and soul-searching that one may think he "finds God."

However, God never left, never moved away—we did, and we spend most of our days living beside ourselves, drifting farther from our true home. He is just waiting for us to come back home. He knows our pain and hurt and failures, but He waits for us to bring it all to Him. Truthfully, you cannot find something that has never been lost; discovery comes into play when we "find" out what has been missing in our lives all along.

The parable of the prodigal son (found in Luke 15:11-32) serves the same life lesson as the parable of the prodigal inmate. "Prodigal," which means radically extravagant, describes the person who behaves with reckless abandon. Hence, it is fair to conclude that we inmates have been prodigal in our actions, which landed us where we are today. However, for most, the parable of the prodigal inmate leaves off where the parable of the prodigal son begins: beside themselves and lost!

In the story of the prodigal son, the son left his father's home, where he was well provided for; but he realized that he was lost, that he was lacking in the world, and that he needed to turn back to his father. What changed? The parable tells us: "But when he came to himself . . . " (Luke 15:17).

The prodigal son "came to himself"—finally realizing that he was the one who was lost, and that he needed to return home. Home—where his father was waiting, where his father had always been and had never left. The prodigal inmate does not "find God"—we find ourselves hurting and realize God is the only one who will help in the time of need.

> **Confined or free, we must have this prodigal attitude, radically extravagant, and with reckless abandon admit that we are the ones who are lost.**

When we finally "come to ourselves," we must arise and go to our Father and say to Him, "Father, I have sinned against heaven and in your sight, and am no longer worthy to be called your son" (Luke 15:21).

My *View Apart* is no longer experiencing life "beside myself," but in drawing ever closer to that which was never lost. And I did so by coming back to myself and back to God, who never left. I missed the first 25 years of my life, living beside myself and prodigal for the wrong reasons; but now confined and at peace, I must be prodigal for Christ. I am His son: I was dead and am alive; I was lost and now am found (Luke 15:24).

15. Ability to Choose

The God-given ability to choose. I chose to get up out of bed this morning at 5:30 A.M. before anyone else was up. I chose to walk to the back of the tier to pray and work out. When the blinding lights came on at 6 A.M., I chose to smile instead of frown at the chronic chaos that can always be anticipated at such an early hour. "Joy comes in the morning" (Psalm 30:5), and it's my choice to embrace it!

Some do not even stir; that's their choice. Many get dressed quickly and rush to mess call, only to return afterward for more sleep; that's their choice—it is not forced on them. I choose to begin each day with the reading and studying of God's Word; nobody else can make that decision for me. I choose to respond in careful and thoughtful detail to the several pieces of mail I receive daily. I hear gossip and slander—tales that are not true, but said out of envy and hate; it's my choice how I respond. Sometimes I fail in my response, reacting out of anger; but I choose the response.

Yard call announced! I choose to go and work out. Tensions are high and competition turns threatening; my choice—no one else's: I choose to walk away.

Back on the tier, and there is nothing to do. The decision is mine: choose to lie down; choose to play cards or watch television; choose to read an insignificant magazine. I choose to read material of substance—essential and meaningful. The choice! I made it. A CO enters the tier and reprimands everyone for the smoke and other nonsense; many grumble and complain at the degrading treatment. I could join in the outcry, but I choose to continue reading.

Lights are turned off at 10:30 P.M.; I can retire to bed and attempt to fall asleep through the clamor or I can flip out and tell those around me to quiet down. Choices. I choose to close my eyes and talk to my Father. I thank Him for the ability to choose.

This environment will devour a person in the same way the devil will devour an individual (I Peter 5:8), but only if the person allows it; it is his choice. I make my choices daily; sometimes they are the wrong choices, but the beauty of a choice—a selection, an option, the power to decide—is that it's up to me. And the next time, I can make the right choice. No one else can choose my attitude or how I respond to life's circumstances; neither can I make those choices for someone else.

However, in prison, sometimes we don't have a choice. They say, "STRIP NAKED!" I must strip. They say, "HANDS ON THE WALL," I must comply for the pat down. They say "LOCK IN!" I have no choice—I lock in. Then again, my choice to submit has one set of results; whereas the opposite choice produces different consequences. It's the God-given ability to choose.

> I choose to be positive over negative. I choose purpose over perplexity. I choose being better over being bitter. I choose responsibility over irresponsibility. I choose to walk by faith rather than by sight. I choose hope over despair.

My *View Apart*: I choose the God-given ability of choice over the enticement of the world's voice. I know I messed up big time, but I choose to recognize it and respond to it. We make choices every day. The choice is ours to make, with no excuses.

The blazing lights are on at 6 A.M. sharp—it's another day in prison. The choice is mine! Smiling and content, I am *Imprisoned by Peace*.

16. Lights Out!

LIGHTS OUT! And it's hard to see what I'm writing, but I hurry to finish what I started about two hours ago. A few distractions here and there, and now the lights are out, and my thoughts are incomplete. There is something about the lights going out in this environment that heightens my awareness, but settles my mind.

The days are long, but they go by quickly if one stays busy—and busy I stay so that, usually, when the lights finally rest, I know that my eyes and mind may follow suit.

LIGHTS OUT! And though I'm at ease, I'm aware. I become completely aware of the day's events as I replay them in my head like a slideshow. This is the relaxing part of my day because at this point I'm no longer trying to figure things out, just evaluating my actions and reactions and how I may do better when the lights resume illuminating.

> **My *View Apart* is that I feel God's peace throughout the days, but there is something special about "Being Still" at rest that makes me completely aware of His presence.**

Extinguishing the lights diminishes most of the chaos and acts as an alarm clock for initiating my time of reflection and rest.

LIGHTS OUT! I'm settled now, but well aware—and just as quick as they go out, they will be coming back on. But not so fast, and not without thanks to Him who guards my heart and mind. This has nothing to do with hastening the day to completion—another day in prison is over—but more a sense of completion as I'm able to consider what that day accomplished in God's plan for my life.

Lord, thank you for the light going out, and thank you for its soon return. Amen.

17. Nothing I Wanted, Everything I Needed

Time has wings behind these walls, and it flies with or without you. It speeds relentlessly onward regardless of the people and situations, and that is why it is crucial to get onboard with the time in order to not miss what it has to offer. I try so very hard to imitate the time with my Christian walk, steady and consistent, knowing that all that happens under time's flight does not happen "to me," but "for me."

I view this place as my peace and perfection: It is nothing I wanted, but everything I needed.

From the people made of sand paper to the circumstances designed for grinding, all alike enter our lives at the right time so that we may use them to smooth out the rough edges of our character. Unfortunately, a lot of time for an inmate is spent talking about what is wanted, as opposed to what is needed. Often, we are confused about the difference between an actual "need" and a "want." A *"need"* is a "necessity or the state of lacking something that is required" versus a *"want,"* which is "to greatly desire or wish for something."

We *want* ease and luxury in life, and we *want* them in our timing.

A prisoner *wants* his time to hurry up, as he waits for it at the finish line. Then, while waiting, he complains about what has happened "to him," missing the refining improvement that was happening "for him." Time, moving inexorably forward, will find its way to an inmate's release date—thereby giving him what he wanted, but his misplaced focus prevented him from getting what he needed.

> My *View Apart* now understands that we ask God through selfish desires for our wants—and then miss His answers as He sends them in the form of what we actually need.

An inmate has no shame in asking another for something that he wants, not a need by any means, but purely a selfish want. It is not uncommon to have someone ask for the candy bar you are eating—not a piece of it, but all of it.

This seemingly trivial scenario always leaves me contemplating how we all are in life at times. We ask for riches and rewards, but when we lose our jobs, we may miss the greater opportunity before us due to our sulking (our misplaced focus). We ask for better patience, and then become bitter in traffic. We are too busy trying to figure out why we were not given what we asked for to realize that what has actually transpired is what we needed. It's time to redeem the time, because with it God will rub the "mess" right out of us. He may give us nothing we wanted, but it will be everything we needed.

I pray for peace, and I receive chaos; I pray to be a light, and I find myself among darkness; I pray to reflect Christ, and I feel rejection and affliction.

Nothing I wanted. Everything I needed! And I thank God for all these answers because they are not happening "to me," they are happening "for me." I do not expect to ever again be in such an environment so I cherish this time. I cherish the grinder, and I cherish the sand paper—because through it all and with time, I am learning to be steady and consistent in my Christian walk.

The truth remains: We *need* struggles in life, for without them we would not see how strong we actually are. We *want* strength, so difficulties are given. We *want* wisdom and discernment, so problems are presented. We *want* liberty, so we are given checks to keep us in balance.

We received nothing we *wanted*, but everything we *needed*!

I cannot complain about a single thing in here; and though I am guilty of asking God for so many selfish wants, I am thankful that He always gives me what I need.

18. A Prisoner's Plea and Prayer

I signed one plea bargain prior to this incarceration, which placed my fate in the hands of the system. Left to the judge's discretion in my case, I received five-and-a-half years—required to serve a minimum of 85 percent under federal sentencing laws. Now, according to the State, I am considered many things based on this plea agreement. But had I not recognized by the grace of God that I had another plea in me, I would not be where I am today: spiritually and mentally free.

My *View Apart* offers up another plea—a plea for forgiveness; and this new plea agreement, which places my fate in the hands of God, tells me who, where, and what I really am! "But by the grace of God I am what I am, and His grace toward me was not in vain; but I labored more abundantly than they all, yet not I, but the grace of God which was with me" (I Corinthians 15:10).

I did not intend for this crime to happen, but I caused it. Now I am reacting to my cause by the grace of God. My past will attempt to destroy my future—people will continue to talk; people will continue to hate—but God's grace will so much more abound. "Moreover the law entered that the offense might abound. But where sin abounded, grace abounded much more" (Romans 5:20).

> **I am inadequate, but the Lord's strength is made perfect in my weakness.**

I can take one day at a time—no more and no less—as the grace of God is sufficient for me. "And He said to me, 'My grace is sufficient for you, for My strength is made perfect in weakness'" (II Corinthians 12:9).

This is my prisoner's prayer:

"To God be the glory in all that I do;
A Prisoner's Prayer, when all things become new.
But old things must pass, in order to see;
A prayer of thanks to Him who made me.
So let me begin, from a spirit not constrained,
A Prisoner's Prayer, in Jesus' name:
Though incarcerated, I am set free;
Not from struggle outside, but through struggle in me.
Though physically confined, I remain at peace.
Authority may be theirs, but my mind is at ease.
Though imprisoned, I count it all blessing;
For by various trials, my faith stands the testing.
Though a convict on paper, I will not slow my pace;
Convicted by Christ, I must finish the race.
A Prisoner's Prayer, by purpose I'm driven;
This too shall pass, for true is my vision."

My plea and prayer are made possible only by the grace of God. I know who, where, and what I am in the present; and by His grace, He has forgiven who, where, and what I was in the past.

According to the State, I am Inmate 314525E, but I know who I am—a child of God. Currently, I am considered property of the Department of Corrections at Mid-State Prison, but I know where I am—a state of grace. My face sheet (my prisoner information) declares that I am a violent offender, but I know what I am—forgiven.

19. The World of Questions

You want peace of mind and livin', here's a piece of mine from prison: Questions upon questions upon questions, but never the answer we are looking for. Perhaps we are asking the wrong questions; perhaps we already know the right answer. This world is the world of questions, and we seek the answer from this world. As I contemplate such thoughts, my *View Apart* finds the answer through confinement—but few would choose to seek the answer in this "world." Here is my riddle: In honor of the "world of answers," and to put to shame the world of questions, I will present multiple questions that all have the same answer.

This isn't a church, cathedral, seminary or monastery and it's certainly not a vacation, but this answer comes from prison. Amongst evil. Amongst distress. Amongst chaos. Amongst ignorance. Amongst turmoil.

How can one wake up with joy where the environment moans in constant lament? How can one remain at peace when chaos rules the conditions? How can one see this place as a step up (an opportunity to improve) and not a step back? How is time served not time lost? How can one fear no evil? How is one confined, yet free? How can one see light in the dark? How can one move forward, when the world wants to remind them of their backward past? Who can explain this?

The answer: The answer is "The Joy," the answer is "The Peace," the answer is "The Planner," the answer is "The Time Keeper," the answer is "The Comfort," the answer is "The Savior," the answer is "The Light," the answer is "The Redeemer," the answer is God.

> **Without God, we will continue to live in the world of questions without answers.**

20. Prison Is an Island

Prison is an island where provisions are limited. I arrived at this island by myself, by willful choice and by even more willful ignorance. I sailed past the lifeboats, believing I knew better than the "life" offered on those boats. When I had been secure on land, I had all I ever needed—but I did not grasp the worth of all that I had beneath me, around me, and (most crucially) what was offered above me.

I did not heed the "life preserver" pushing against my heart.

The land was abundant, and provisions were plentiful; yet I misused all that was given to me. While I possessed it all, I believed I did so by my own doing—and congratulated myself on my successes.

I needed to be RELOCATED

To get RECONNECTED;

I needed to be DISPLACED

To find HIS PLACE!

Prison is an island, and I will remain here until I am mature enough to say, "There is-land and it's *His*-land!" God required my undivided attention, so division from the land was necessary and warranted. But now set apart from land, I am finding the ground I stand on and the isolation around me to be the "saving grace" that I needed. I did not view the former land in the right way nor was I careful in observing the fruit of the land for my picking. I thought I was safe on that land or afloat in my "unsinkable" boat.

My *View Apart* now sees that this island is for my protection and purpose, "to humble and test [me], to know what was in [my] heart" (Deuteronomy 8:2). I used to live off the land and its bread, but on this island (*His*-land) "He humbled [me], allowed [me] to hunger, and fed [me] with manna which [I] did not know . . . that He might make [me] know that man shall not live by bread alone; but man lives by every word that proceeds from the mouth of the Lord" (Deuteronomy 8:3).

On this island, I've found everything that I will ever need; and though I am surrounded by a sea of prison bars and barbed wire, I finally see there is-land and have placed that side of the sea in *His*-hand. Detained on this island, I am content.

> **This isolation is for my transformation, and God already knows my destination.**

"For the Lord [my] God is bringing [me] into a good land" (Deuteronomy 8:7) from this island!

Prison is an island, but my *View Apart* knows that this is-land does not have to be a prison.

21. When Darkness Comes

I awake in a dark prison, yet I am free—a light apart from darkness. But the darkness exists, and I have learned that it is better to wake up in dark circumstances with God's presence than to wake up alone in presumed light.

> **Even in times of trials amid darkness, when one is with God, the lessons gained and the understanding attained are deeper than that which is learned in the pretentious light.**

"I have learnt to love the darkness of sorrow; there you see the brightness of His face."[1] How can one "love the darkness of sorrow"? I asked myself this same question; then I realized the importance of the word "learned" in the beginning of the quote. We may "learn" to always have a *View Apart*, even when darkness comes.

Learn: to acquire knowledge or understanding; to be informed; to find out; to memorize.

Learning requires a decision to do so, a drive for information, a determination to understand, a desire to become skilled. In all our situations, something may be learned; but in which direction do we head while lost in the darkness of sorrow—farther into the darkness or into God's brightness? When I look around in my environment I easily perceive the "darkness of sorrow" on so many faces. The sorrow could serve as their teacher, yet many learn the wrong lesson.

Often, in the darkness, we try to find our own way by relying on ourselves or the wrong guidance. We rush about rather than "Be Still" in the darkness. This frenzy impairs the refining process and offers no relief. When darkness comes, it is for our needed repairs and offers perfect relief—through the learned response of seeking "the brightness of God's face"!

It took prison for me to learn the truth of this revelation, but it just goes to show you that the brightness of God's face can be seen anywhere—when we learn to yield to Him when darkness comes. With my *View Apart*, I see clearly that the light may be shrouded, but the covering is for our benefit as we learn to trust God in the darkness. We must learn to love our painful circumstances and use them to feel God's peace, mercy, and grace. Experience is the greatest teacher, and even when the light at the end of the proverbial tunnel cannot be seen, God promises: "I will make darkness light before them" (Isaiah 42:16).

However, the absence of darkness and trials does not necessarily indicate blessing. In fact, it is in the captivity of darkness that we are able to see God's blessing more clearly. It is in "learn[ing] to love the darkness" that our hearts and minds are opened, as God opens His arms. "I will be found by you, says the Lord, and I will bring you back from your captivity" (Jeremiah 29:14).

In learning to love the darkness of sorrow, you will see the brightness of God's face. Learn the lessons now, for darkness shall come!

22. By Faith, I Understand

Faith is a touchy subject in prison, where many insist that something must be touched to believe that it exists. When faith is mentioned or brought up among inmates, it's as if it is just a name of a country singer—and a hill they do not desire to climb. But this climb they never venture to experience is that which would save their lives, for by faith God takes us up and through any circumstance.

Just an everyday walk through the prison and out into the yard reveals that faith no longer has to be a touchy subject. Our surroundings alone show us faith in sight, faith in hearing, and faith in feeling.

Leaving the prison tier, it is a requirement that inmates walk through one of the many assigned metal detectors. This is to prevent them from bringing a shank (prison-made knife or dagger) or other weapon into the various areas of the general population. As I walk through this metal detector, I can see the arched structure that frames my body on both sides and over my head; but I cannot see nor can I feel the power emanating from the structure, which is capable of detecting metal. By faith, I accept the reality that the unseen certainly detects metal.

Once into the open prison yard, I often use my personal AM/FM radio to tune in to music. I hold the radio in my hand and place the ear-buds into my ears. Once again, I cannot see the invisible radio waves signaling to my device, but I can certainly hear what is coming through; and by faith, I understand that the unseen certainly transmits music.

Even on a hot day, there is a slight breeze. The prison yard is a large square, and three of its sides are blocked in: one by the prison itself, and two sides are backed by thick woods; but the fourth side has a slight clearing, which allows the wind to blow across the yard. I cannot see the wind, yet I feel it; and I can see its effects in the trees: the rustling of the leaves, and the waving of the branches. By faith, I know that the unseen certainly moves and has a presence.

This same hot day has another witness that testifies for faith. I am able to feel the heat from the sun, but I cannot see the ultraviolet rays that penetrate my skin and cause a reaction. I know the rays can brown (tan) or redden (sunburn) skin because I can see those effects; and by faith, I comprehend that the unseen certainly changes my complexion.

Without a shadow of a doubt, some things exist and are real whether we can see them or feel them or hear them or taste them or touch them—or not. In all of these familiar activities, inmates do not doubt because we take the effects as the evidence of things not seen. We cannot always fully experience through our senses the source that provides the substance, but we trust in the source and know it is real. By faith, I believe in the unseen: the currents that detect the metal; the waves that transmit the music; the winds that move the trees; the rays that warm and color our skin.

> **By faith, I believe in the unseen: God; His love; His grace; His peace. I cannot see these things, but I know they are real because I experience their effects.**

And it is by faith that the unseen becomes my *View Apart*! By faith I understand why I have such peace though confined.

How many times throughout our days do we demonstrate trust in the unseen? Faith in God is no different as our life actually depends on it. There remains no reason for it to be a touchy subject, when we don't even allow it to touch our hearts and minds. When we place our faith in God, He will protect us like the metal detector, speak to us like the radio, touch us like the wind, and shine upon us like the sun.

23. Real Freedom

An inmate spends many of his imprisoned days desiring to be free, and in most cases the fulfillment of this longing is a long way off. This craving for freedom causes inmates to miss the lessons set before them, as well as the opportunity to have real freedom before their physical freedom becomes real. Yet one "look-over" in this environment would be enough to convince a person that it is the norm to "stay-under" his circumstances. However, I spend a lot of my incarcerated time contemplating thoughts that go against the norm for an imprisoned man, but "as he thinks in his heart, so is he" (Proverbs 23:7).

I must go against the norm again and declare that even if I could leave prison tomorrow, I wouldn't. I know that the work being done within me behind these walls far outweighs a premature deliverance. I have made this claim numerous times prior and not by my own accord, but according to Christ who lives in me: "I do not desire to be free: I *am* free."

"You can open a rosebud, but you spoil the flower."[1] Beautiful roses are being strangled in here daily by the thorns of their own longing. While my fellow inmates wish for liberty and a better future upon release, they do not allow the time for real freedom to blossom within them. All forms of growth, meta-morphosis or transformation take time—and not our time, but His time: the One who controls the rising of the sun and the going down of the same.

> **Wanting to be free while confined is natural, but being free while confined is supernatural.**

"Christ has made us free" (Galatians 5:1).

This *View Apart* has allowed me to reconsider my ways, my passions, my convictions and beliefs. Previously, I depended on the freedom around me and the possessions before me. Now I realize that real freedom is based on the Spirit inside me and what Christ did before me. As Richard Wurmbrand relates[2]:

> The tyrant of Syracuse once went to the slave philos-opher, Epictetus, and told him, "I'll pay the ransom for you, and you will be liberated."
>
> Epictetus replied, "Why do you care about me? Free yourself."
>
> "But I am a king," said the amazed tyrant.
>
> "This I contest," was the answer of the philosopher. "He who masters his passions (and thoughts) is a king even while in chains. He who is ruled by his passions (and thoughts) is a slave even while sitting on a throne."
>
> Real freedom does not depend upon external cir-cumstances. There exists the wonderful liberty of which

the children of God partake, even when in straitened circumstances or trammeled by prison walls.

Therefore I say again, I do not desire to be free. I am free already. These prison walls stopped life as I knew it, when I knew nothing. Within these prison walls, Jesus has given me life as I know it; and I "have it more abundantly" (John 10:10). Real freedom is a choice that cannot be contained or confined. These prison walls would agree, if they could talk!

24. Buried to Live

I am incarcerated. I am dead and buried, as most inmates and even society thus consider a prisoner. This isolation from the world has set me apart from the material conditions that I once loved so well. Nevertheless, time exists for me as it exists for the civilizations outside this prison. This is certain! How we are able to use this gift of time differs by the external in which we live (the setting) and the internal on which we live (the heart). Now I realize that being dead and buried to the world isn't so bad after all. In fact, I have been buried to live!

The world may be boundless in what it can do, and I may be bound to what I cannot do, but God's time abounds when we give Him what's due!

As the world's time passes and I find myself out of sight and thus out of mind, I find great significance in being dead to the world. Like a seed that is buried in the ground, I must die before I sprout forth and live again. The world would believe I'm buried, but God would call it "planted." As my time and the world's time moves concurrently, God grows His way what the world thinks is thrown away! It's a *View Apart*: I am dead to the world, but buried to live!

People tend to take their freedom for granted (physical freedom), but my time is spent in a freedom I won't forget (spiritual). The world's time sees depreciation; but with my time, I have learned appreciation.

> God gives us external time to change our internal mind, so that we may spend with Him eternal time.

"Foolish one, what you sow is not made alive unless it dies" (1 Corinthians 15:36). I am planted so that I may bear fruit the proper way. I set myself in the wrong soil with the wrong nourishment when I was free outside. Now confined and at peace inside, I do not grieve being dead to the world—for in this death, I have been buried to live! I am planted for His purpose, so that I may not return to the world useless, ineffectual, and vain.

25. The Past is Knocking

I would have literally flown off the handle in here countless times had it not been for Christ in my life. Formerly, I would have answered to the many knocks on my ego in such a way that this incarceration would have turned quickly into devastation. I realize that if the "me in me," which is the very flesh that I am made of, has his way on a daily basis, then I am nothing but my past conviction: aggravated manslaughter. This past I am not proud of, but this past I am not, and I now have a new core conviction that has made me a new creation: the Christ in me.

Still, the past continues to knock. "Does Matthew Maher live here?" inquires the past. "No," I answer, "he died. Christ lives here now. So go away."

> **And with the past leaving, the future awaits.**

I know that any good I may ever do is the Christ in me, and any wretchedness done is the "me in me." I know this well because I have seen the "me in me" in action. The "me in me" must die daily for the Christ in me to live. The "me in me" pushes my fellow man away and does not want to be bothered, but the Christ in me welcomes him in. The "me in me" is covered in sin, but the Christ in me smothers sin.

My *View Apart* recognizes that in prison, I am free with the Christ in me; and to be free with just the "me in me" is a prison. If the "me in me" answers the knock at the door, he will easily let the past back in— blocking the present and disregarding the future; that is why I must allow the Christ in me to have His perfect way. The "me in me" did not care for this house, but the Christ in me has called me His home. I must not allow the "me in me" to win, for when the "me in me" wins, I lose.

I am no longer alone in this confinement. The past knows this, but he knocks anyway. The past knows how weak the "me in me" is, but that was before the Christ moved in. The "me in me" is weak, but the Christ in me is strong. I am not anxious over the death of the "me in me," because with the Christ in me I have never felt more alive. I must move on as the "me in me" moves out; for when the Christ in me takes ownership, none of these hard-knocks of life will move me.

Still, the knocks continue and I am one answer away from a fall. KNOCK! KNOCK! Pride. Anger. Selfishness. Greed. "Open up," they demand.

There will be so many more knocks at my door, but the "me in me" no longer has the right to answer. Though the "me in me" may want to respond, "it is no longer [the "me in me"] who lives, but Christ lives in me" (Galatians 2:20).

KNOCK! KNOCK!

"Who's there?"

"It's me! Let me back in!"

"No, Christ lives here now."

"Did I say 'me'? I mean 'It's YOU.' Now open the door!"

I cannot live with the "me in me" lest I cause any more pain. The past is knocking, but "the man of this house" refuses to answer so the Son of Man can lead the way.

26. Stumbling Blocks and Stepping Stones

Regardless of the status of my relationship with various inmates, I am always delighted when I hear they are going home soon. I have encountered so many different types of perspectives, views, and outlooks from the soon-to-be-released inmates, but all have one thing in common as they approach their long-awaited freedom: All alike seek release from the fear of failure.

Every inmate, who is going home, needs affirmation from his peers that everything is going to be all right. Motivated by this oppressive worry, he is anxious to talk about his impending release. Selfishly, however, most inmates do not want to entertain that thought or hear that conversation.

I, on the other hand, never mind lending this ear of mine to that boast of home because it allows for me to present the topic of faith in God. Usually, it is not quite the response the inmate was seeking, but it almost always leads to the next reality—which are the obstacles one must face upon release. Sadly, no amount of encouragement is able to overcome an outlook of defeat; so despite an imminent release date, many fall backward before they even begin their new journey beyond these prison walls.

An inmate who is departing these gates is granted a fresh start. He can take one day at a time. Easier said or written about than done, of course. But the unknown outside these walls does not have to vanquish an inmate's joy upon release.

Personally, I do not know what to expect when I am closing in on my own release date, but I do know that the only job that starts at the top is digging a hole. I have committed my perspective to a *View Apart*; and though stumbling blocks and hardships await my arrival, I am confident there will also be stepping stones gained from this experience.

We can never assume that things in life will be a certain way because of our past experiences or past stumbles; ultimately, the past will be what we make of it, especially if we use it to better ourselves. Still, as an inmate, I can see how there is another element of the unknown thrown into our equation. The label we carry, the shame, the regret, and so much more can be daunting for the majority and make the future a frightening proposition.

As I think back on my own life, however, I realize that nothing is what I originally thought. I am now fully aware that some of my stepping stones turned out to be stumbling blocks; and some of my stumbling blocks turned out to be stepping stones. At first view, I believed many of my failures were setbacks, but that is because I failed to view them as setups.

> **The difference between stumbling blocks and stepping stones, setbacks and setups is how we use them!**

Nothing makes sense to me these days except my faith in God. I know that "all things [even stumbling blocks] work together for good to those who love God, to those who are called according to His purpose" (Romans 8:28).

There is value in listening to the homeward-bound inmates ruminate on their anticipated freedom, and it is important to offer affirmation, but the confidence boost must be accepted and then applied. Stumbling blocks or stepping stones—it all depends on how one views them and how one uses them. My release day shall come too, and I'm taking this inner freedom out with me, for being *Imprisoned by Peace* has nothing to do with a location.

27. If These Prison Walls Could Talk

I know I have seen way more than my eyes could handle during my time imprisoned, and with my observations come crazy contemplations. So I wonder: If my eyes have seen so much, what have these walls witnessed over their extended stay? They stand strong year after year, as the environment remains consistent to its occupants: felonious. If these prison walls could talk, I wonder: What would they say?

I doubt anybody has even cared that these walls have been listening, nor would the suggestion to ask for their opinions ever actually take place. But if, like the enchanted apple trees in *The Wizard of Oz*, they could respond, would they report on the continual folly and boredom that takes place or would they delve deeper than that? Perhaps they would like to talk about the atmospheric change and pressure release that they are beginning to feel. I could imagine they would be so used to listening to empty words, caustic language, and far-fetched dreams that anything contradictory to the prison vernacular would cause their ears to tingle. So I continue to wonder: If these walls could talk, what would they say?

The accumulated weight of illusory wishes and ignorant intentions has had its way within these walls for too long. Possibly, the walls would argue that the stiff and stubborn mold pasted so vigorously on them may break up and fall away in a different culture. If these prison walls could talk, they may claim that their mold of concrete mortar makes them who they are; and to get along within, one must conform to their standards. For once out, words cannot be taken back; and there must be some way of containment for the corruption that lives within these walls.

> **My *View Apart* perceives that I am formed by a different mold, where I am the clay and God is the potter.**

He fashions and shapes me as He sees fit. These walls cannot claim dominance over me. Though they impose their confinement, I will no longer allow them to hear idle chat, evil exaltation, devious planning, and hot-air promises. My mouth sings a different song.

Truthfully, I believe in these walls and what they stand for, but they have been misunderstood for too long. They stand for protection, not disconnection. They stand for isolation, not rehabilitation. Isolation and protection bring the pain out for its healing; whereas, the rehabilitation must be personal and is not the walls' responsibility.

But just for fun, I would ask the walls, "How do you feel?" And if these prison walls could talk, they might say:

"I've spent all my time within these tiers, whose influence is this which has reached my ears?

I once stood up against the times, but too much pressure and too much crime!

I must admit the change feels nice; but please, kind sir, there must be a price?"

To which, I would reply:

"You talk, Prison Walls? They definitely won't believe me now; but if you denounce your ways, I'll tell you how.

The influence is God's, and it did come with a price: One that was willfully paid by Jesus' life.

He created all things, and in Him we are found. Prison Wall, you may be standing up, but to Him you'll bow down.

Walls, you don't stand in my way; I'm as free as a bird and in Jesus I pray."

SLAM!!!

I'd wake up to the slamming of the prison gate; and I would still wonder: If these prison walls could talk, what would they say? If these prison walls could talk, in them I believe I've found a friend.

28. Time in Humility

I am humbled to be on this journey called confinement, and broken for the same reason. It is not somewhere I would ever have seen myself, not in a million years, but we only see the worldly perspective. I still awake and sometimes the present moment seems surreal, but regardless of the dream-like feelings, I know this peace is real. I see things differently now, and it is a *View Apart* that has only come by way of being set apart. I will forever be remorseful for what I've done, and I certainly deserved punishment and correction, but I would be a fool if I didn't use this time for acknowledgment and reflection. What is revealed is what I needed to know, if not what I wanted to experience!

Prison can be a blessing for any inmate because it's an opportunity to recognize one's failures, faults, and flaws and deal with them accordingly. Yet many do not identify this time away as anything but an inconvenience. Instead of valuing this time as a humbling new beginning, they continue on in their old ways as if their former lives are on "pause" instead of at an end.

> I will never get this chance again to be refined while confined and though the world shuns those in prison, God will honor those who honor Him and honor His time.

The world wants me to sit and sulk, but I refuse. The world is pleased to see me here—and I agree for I am right where I am supposed to be. I know all too well how busy the other side of these walls can be, so it would be disgraceful of me if I did not apply this time in a correctional facility—or better put, time in humility. It's not how high you can get, but how low you can go "[f]or He brings down those who dwell on high" (Isaiah 26:5). I was the chief of pride, but now I know that it is pride that keeps us weak. I needed this time in humility, that I may cause no more pain. "God resists the proud, but gives grace to the humble" (James 4:6).

29. More Than Words

How can I best express this *View Apart*? After re-reading these contemplations, I realize they are mere words on paper and not my actual experience. Even if I were able to accurately depict my personal experiences using the most appropriate words and figurative language, there would still be so much more left unsaid. Thousands upon thousands of thoughts can be inspired from one scenario; so a great deal is left out, and I feel that my writing will always be left wanting.

Even as you read this contemplation, know that my words are one thing, but the blank spaces between the words are entirely another. Just as when we are told to "read between the lines" because there is more to an expression than meets the eye, likewise there is much more to these experiences behind bars. Therefore, you must read between the lines.

Words can evoke images and emotions; and when shared properly, they are powerful enough to ignite motivation, inspiration, consideration, contemplation, transformation, and so much more. If words are capable of accomplishing so much, then consider the potential that lies in the spaces between them—which are the actual experiences themselves. More than words!

We are less likely to take somebody's "word for it" unless they have credibility through experience. I would offer more in these contemplations if I knew how, but no amount of words can properly express this confined peace so you must take my wholehearted "word for it" that what is shared is more than words.

If I am able to express strength through these words, it is crucial to understand that the words are merely symbolic of the strength displayed in the actual experience—which takes place in the space between the words.

> Yet, in that space between the words, you would also be able to see my weaknesses—and then you would comprehend that "[God's] strength is made perfect in weakness" (2 Corinthians 12:9).

I share my heart and mind through Christ, in hope that these words may challenge your spiritual growth. I am writing from the belly of the beast, but this peace keeps me assured that freedom does not depend on external circumstances but on how the internal allows Christ to reign. I can only share these experiences in words, but you must understand that they are much more than mere words. These words may be read, but the experiences were lived; and the result is a *View Apart*!

30. "I Can" Even in a Trash Can

I can. I will. I must.

> **Regardless of my circumstances, "I can do all things through Christ who strengthens me" (Philippians 4:13)—a truth finally grasped by me, better late than never.**

And now I sit in a prison, attempting to clean up what I've messed up, knowing that this is also better late than never. I know where I am and where these thoughts and passions have been awakened, and—to its credit—confinement has been the path necessary for God to turn my trash to treasure.

A politician once said, "Prison is the place where society throws all of the trash that it collects in hopes of cleaning up the communities." I am now in this "trash can," and I agree that garbage must be removed from the streets. But I would like to pose a question in response: What happens to the trash in this can? With no attempts made to clean up the trash in the can, what might my "trash can" experience produce?

If I am considered trash, then I compare myself to a cigarette. I have been tossed into the bin while still lit. One must be very careful when placing anything flammable in the trash. A cigarette may enter the can seemingly snuffed out and unusable, but one spark in the trash can ignites a fire that will not only consume the surrounding garbage but is capable of burning down the whole house. Had the cigarette butt been placed in an ashtray or extinguished, there would have been no fire. My *View Apart* knows that the "trash can" experience for this half-lit cigarette proved to be the perfect environment for a fire to be set ablaze—for without any of the elements and conditions surrounding me, my smoldering ash of faith would have burned out neglected in a gilded container. "A bruised reed He will not break, and smoking flax He will not quench; He will bring forth justice for truth" (Isaiah 42:3).

I can. I will. I must clean up what I've messed up. Regardless of being in a "can," I CAN do all things through Christ who strengthens me—even in a TRASH CAN.

31. Freedom Side

Prison visits are both a gift and a curse. They are a gift because the inmate gets to see family and friends and feel their support; but they are equally a curse because the inmate is left feeling once again the impact of loss—loss of his loved ones, and loss of liberty because he cannot do what they can do: go back to the "free side." Most inmates, at the conclusion of the visits, find themselves standing strong in line formation—blowing kisses and flashing waves to their visitors, assuring them that everything is going to be all right. Then the inmates must return to their side. What the visitors are spared is the scene after the gate closes behind the inmates—when those same strong standers are now broken down and stranded. Alone on this side of freedom—the side where nobody desires to be. Alone on this island amidst a sea of harsh emotions.

However, I have found my visits to be quite the opposite experience of most of the general population—not because *I* am any stronger than the next man, but because I know from Whom my strength and peace come. Most of the visitation time with my friends and family is spent catching up with life on both sides of freedom, their side and my side. I spend a lot of the time trying to explain my side of the wall—the view that they should never see; but I know I must do my best to share what I have learned about my side of freedom.

This side of freedom for me is true freedom and true peace. For it is through the unexpected confinement of my body that my soul has been set free! It's more than a feeling. Neither do I insist on this view for their sakes, for their peace of mind. I simply must stay true to my core convictions of heart and mind that now see life on a different playing field. A belief that assures me this physical prison is temporary, but the mental and spiritual freedom that I have obtained is forever. And forever is not just a long time.

My mind no longer recognizes this side of freedom as bondage. My mind is not delusional, but delighted. "Delight yourself also in the Lord, and He shall give you the desires of your heart" (Psalm 37:4).

I am on the side of freedom that many will never understand, as they believe themselves to be on the right side, the "free side." But being able to walk out of prison after a visit does not make one free.

> **Truthfully, on whatever side the Lord is invited is the right side, the freedom side.**

Visits for me have never been a time to show face, but a time to show Christ. I am here to repay a debt that I can never cover on my own. Thus, the peace of God that I know and feel was paid in full and bought at a price—forgiveness and salvation from sin through the death and resurrection of Jesus Christ. This is true life and liberty.

My visitors return to their freedom on the outside and I return to my confinement on the inside, but ultimately the side that offers true freedom is the one with the *View Apart* that starts at the heart.

The sliding metal gate separates the inmates from their lifelines on the other side. They are alone again. The air does not breathe in the same way—this is the curse part of the visit. I gaze around and see so many countenances of desolation reflecting the unspoken agreement that this is the wrong side of freedom to be on. I can only bow my head in these moments and pray.

"O Lord, that I may bless You indeed. That You would show my companions that the freedom side is wherever You reside. That You would fall on me, fill in me, and be felt through me—that all may experience this peace from You. O Lord, as I return to the side that is right in Your sight, I thank You for this confined peace; that You would keep me from evil; and that I may cause no more pain. No more pain, Lord God. Amen."

32. Inside Out

I can't see my own inside, but I desire to show my inside out. This backfires at times as what comes out is not always lined up with what I think is on the inside. It's a battle I can't win, but one that God uses to show me what is actually inside of me. This process I have come to appreciate, not because I enjoy being exposed to the "wickedness of my heart," but because it is necessary that I see the dirt *out* that I believed was safe *in*. I want to be clean in and not just clean out, so I must let the Lord clean out what I have hidden within, in order for Him to use me out. Inside out, that is!

"For the Lord does not see as man sees; for man looks at the outward appearance, but the Lord looks at the heart" (I Samuel 16:7). It is typical for us as humans to judge things based on what it looks like from the outside. We are very quick to make our opinions just by appearances—assessments done daily and continually in the prison environment. I've learned that many inmates with a rough-and-tough exterior are as soft as silk stuffing on the inside. Likewise, several inmates come off as put together and presentable, yet they are a miserable wreck on the inside. We should not evaluate anything or anyone based on the exterior.

We were taught as children not to judge a book by its cover. A book with a bland, unappealing or dingy cover doesn't mean that it's not filled with beautiful truths. The same goes for an extremely attractive person—his or her appearance does not signify the absence of internal distress. Personally, it takes a lot for me to show emotional pain, so it is very hard for family and friends to know how to read me. If I am hurting deep down inside and I don't make it known, I have learned that I am only confining myself emotionally. I cannot even help others in a just and honest manner until I have focused attention on the needs of my own heart. When my inside and outside match, then I can assist and relate to other people.

If we flipped a lot of things inside out, we would see the hidden mess. The exposure would show us what needs to be fixed. Once we realize for ourselves that change needs to start from within, we will lift the emotional confinement, which has so many of us captive. We tend to bottle up a lot of issues, causing them to consume our thoughts and negatively affect our actions; and for an inmate, it is a double confinement. It is best when people can see our insides out: the sum of our hearts exposed. Then we genuinely know what we are dealing with, and we can begin to work on solutions.

As I entered into this incarceration, I envisioned that prison had come a long way from the days of inmates busting rocks or slaving on chain gangs. From the outside, I thought

I had prison's pulse. In the 21st Century, there would certainly be more productivity for prisoners than ever before—this was my assumption of the way the prison system worked on the inside. Unfortunately, I learned that looks can be deceiving and assumptions can be wrong—a *View Apart*, from the inside out!

I can confidently say that no matter your situation, your circumstances or your confinement, change must begin from within. Those on the outside may never see the inside of this place, but I refuse to be on the inside in vain—that the Lord may use me from the inside out, for He alone sees my heart and He may expose it as He pleases.

I choose to share what I have seen from the inside out—done so never to judge or condemn what's broken, but only to display the light that I have found within. This light I must let shine, and show the peace that was granted while confined. This peace has set me free. Likewise, God shows us out what is in, in order for us to see what needs to be changed or cherished, fixed or favored. It is never done to harm us, but to show us what is actually inside of us.

> **God allows our insides out because faith that is not tested and exposed cannot be trusted and showed!**

The deeper meaning of this confinement is not about the outward appearance, but it is about what God knows exists in the heart of man. He changes those who are willing to show the inside out for His glory.

33. The Kiss and Dagger

If words are weapons, then this word is the dagger of words in the legal system. It is the kiss of Judas, the knife of Brutus, and once applied its ruthless trace is telling. In all cases involved, it is too late when the willful intent signified by this word is realized because the damage is already inflicted. Although this word finally describes the action done, it also sheds light into the mind of the individual with a "PREMEDITATION" mindset. Inmates who have committed premeditated acts are usually sly in approach and cunning in behavior. They "play the angles"; meaning, they already have the coveted end result figured out long before they begin to work a specific strategy.

For a minor example, but very revealing of the premeditation mindset, consider this behavior. I have witnessed inmates initiate friendships with other inmates based exclusively on their "new friend's" release date. In this situation, the only desired outcome on the part of the initiator is inheriting the personal belongings of the inmate who is leaving. Traditionally, when an inmate is released, these items are left behind for fellow inmates in his circle. A premeditated act such as this one requires at least a week and quite often several weeks to plot out. Actions that are calculated in advance (with a specific, undisclosed outcome in mind) are often devious in nature and ultimately self-serving. Whether the words and actions used in the scheme are as soft and gentle as a kiss or as covert and swift as the thrust of a dagger, the devastating result of betrayal is the same.

Such a powerful word, premeditation: inspired contemplation on the level of determination we as humans exhibit when we really want a specific result, reward or outcome in the end. The amount of time, energy, and brainpower we expend trying to orchestrate in advance some sort of personal benefit or gain can resemble sheer obsessive madness. The selfish ambition behind all the forethought makes our subtle kisses and sharp daggers capable of accomplishing much.

Imagine, then, that we took this word—premeditation—back and applied it for a good purpose. Employing the same resolute determination and firmness of mind, how much more would be accomplished within the boundaries of God's will?

Observing certain behaviors in prison is teaching me a lot about human nature.

> **When our minds are set on something, we push beyond obstacles with deliberate intent and do whatever it takes to ensure our plan is carried out.**

I am convinced as I move forward that it is definitely possible to be a positive "premeditated person." Like the tender touch of a kiss and the piercing affect of a dagger, we can premeditate for a virtuous end rather than for an evil aim. That which I design, ponder or dedicate for God's purposes will inevitably direct me to the right path and enable me to fulfill His perfect plan for my life.

Hence, I began writing with premeditation—knowing that if God remains at the center, He takes good pleasure in seeing His plan carried out for higher purposes. Each of these shared contemplations has been determinedly calculated in advance. Like the kiss of Judas, which was a premeditated act that was predetermined by God to use for His purpose, I too desire "this kiss" to caress the soul of the reader for God's glory, honor, and praise. And like the dagger, I represent that "the word of God is living and powerful, and sharper than any two-edged sword, piercing even to the division of soul and spirit, and of joints and marrow, and is a discerner of the thoughts and intents of the heart" (Hebrews 4:12).

This *View Apart* has allowed me to see the reverse definition of such a powerful word as premeditation—premeditated for HIM, by HIM, and through HIM.

34. Different Sight and Different Sites

It seems like only yesterday that I saw the beginning of this journey. My sight has seen so much from then to now, and it's only natural that I should try to see the end. However, without the sites along the way that inspired my *View Apart*, I could have easily missed the significance of the journey. If I had always been looking at how much longer I had to go, I would have been missing the lessons in the moment. It is during the course—*en route*—that we progress and advance, that we *grow*, when we view with a different sight each different site.

> Regardless of our circumstances in life, too many times we only live for the destination, always looking ahead and striving to get ahead—instead of embracing the different sites along the way.

By sight, I site-see!

We are always in a rush, always seeking the next level, always too busy moving, and life quickly passes us by. Though we may arrive at our destination, we soon realize that it isn't what we thought it would be. We worry about making a living instead of making a life; similarly, a prisoner spends untold time and energy during his incarceration looking ahead to his release, while missing this time set apart to "Be Still."

A *View Apart* does not chase an end, a result or a higher level of status without cherishing the now. I have learned to be thankful along this journey as each new site is encountered, knowing that with each "stop" is an opportunity to "[b]e still and know that [He is] God" (Psalm 46:10). I am focused and in preparation for what lies ahead—the end of confinement—but the journey cannot be ignored. Now I see clearly, and my different sight appreciates the different sites along the way. Each and every conversation, each and every interaction, and each and every situation have been "rest stops" on the road of prison for the refining of my character.

I could have chosen to go in several different directions with this time; I could have closed my eyes to the surroundings and my ears to the call of God. Instead, this site and all the sites have been the sight that fuels my passion: Had I not seen this confinement, I would not have seen true freedom.

Each of our journeys in life is different, but when we take the time to site-see and embrace the moment for all it is worth, we will find ourselves at our destination with an abundance of memories and truths that were there to be cherished.

35. Which View

The "woe is me" mentality is dominant in prison, where most inmates believe they have had an injustice done against them that is responsible for their presence here. Many refuse to see past their own selfishness and sadness, thereby missing the reality that whatever they have done has affected more than just them. It is the tunnel vision of prison to be steadfastly focused on oneself; selfishness reigns, and each person sits on the throne of his own extremely narrow viewpoint.

Through the view of this world, one complains: "O, woe is me as I awake in prison, far from my family and loved ones and among strangers and convicts. I do not belong here for what I've done, and I cannot go on as the time seems to set its pace against me. I do not see an end to this. Dull walls, rusted bars, and filthy floors confine me.

"There are arguments, fights, and ignorance all around me. I have no privacy; I have no silence; I have no tolerance for this place. I lie in bed all day—mind racing, stress dominating. When will this end?

"Nobody understands my pain! Where is my help? Why can't this pass? I close my eyes, and I am still here. I toss and turn, and sleep eludes me. There is no peace. I see no good in this. Woe is me through the view of this world."

> **But there is a *View Apart,* and by it comes the "joy in me" mentality. This throne has the True King sitting upon it and allowing His Word to reign.**

Which view? Well, that's up to *you!*

Through the view of His Word, one proclaims: "There is joy in me as I awake in prison! I belong here for what I have done, and I feel closer to my God and my Savior every day. I press on, as this time is on my side that I may finish this race set before me. With God, I do not need to see an end to this. Dull walls, rusty bars, and filthy floors do not define me.

"Arguments, fights, and ignorance are drowned out to me. I have no privacy—this sharpens me. There is not much silence, so I concentrate harder. My tolerance has greatly grown because of this place. I pray in my spirit all day—mind resting, stress relieving. I do not want this peace to end!

"I now understand what to do with my pain. 'My help comes from the Lord, Who made heaven and Earth' (Psalm 121:2), and this too shall pass. I close my eyes, and I am still (Psalm 46:10). By my patience, my soul I possess (Luke 21:19). I know peace. God will work all these things together for my good because I love Him (Romans 8:28). There is joy in me through the view of His Word."

Two views: "woe is me" and "joy in me." For each view, there is a Supreme Being seated upon the throne of our lives. When we allow Self to reign, selfishness is the game and the view of the world will rule; when we make our hearts God's throne, He makes us His home and the view of His Word will be our perspective. Which view? Well, we have the gift of free will—free will to accept or reject Jesus Christ; free will to choose which view. It's up to you.

36. Set Your Mind's Pace

My eyes are often "running heavy" in this environment, a pace I cannot control, but my mind makes up for this slumberous function by "walking steady." A quiet moment of solitude is rare in prison; when it does occur, it will be brief. During those precious moments, I close my eyes tightly, pressing the muscles together in an attempt to dislodge the weighty heaviness. Soon my eyes must open again, and they are still "running heavy."

The tier is at its quietest when everyone goes to dinner mess. I do not join these mess movements because I eat on my own from canteen. Furthermore, the less time I spend in state khakis, the less I conform to this environment. "Do not be conformed to this world" (Romans 12:2). Additionally, I spend so much time reading and writing that I do not allow the prison's natural movements to break up my productivity and the pace of my mind. "But be transformed by the renewing of your mind."

Many of my fellow inmates tell me that I am working too hard; however, I am working "that [I] may walk worthy of the Lord, fully pleasing Him, being fruitful in every good work and increasing in the knowledge of God" (Colossians 1:10). You see, my *View Apart* is that though my eyes are tired, my mind remains steady; like a walker's stride, I am working to be balanced and consistent.

> **I know that if I can keep my mind set on "being fruitful in every good work," then I may be less likely to stumble or trip.**

When we get ahead of ourselves, like a sprinter who fails to set his pace, we usually become winded earlier than we should have and this affects our balance. We are finished before we finish the race.

I may be prone to fall, but when I am walking steady I am able to recover quicker and easier; I am able to assess and respond to my surroundings immediately and then move forward once again—one step at a time. This entire process of walking steady begins in the mind, because often our eyes may not see things clearly as they are "running" on their own—running ahead or running heavy. I have learned to set my mind's pace by "Being Still"—a discipline that focuses my mind and maintains the determination to stay consistent to the regimen that keeps me on the right track and simultaneously alert to the unexpected hurdles of prison.

Babel and bedlam bustle back in from the mess movement. So many inmates wear themselves out, not with productivity but with rote prison activity. They set their minds' pace to a sprint and soon run out of energy and focus, allowing the prison's movements to move them to dormancy. Any of life's activities have the ability to wear us down as the body is frail, but when we are able to set our minds' pace to "walk worthy of the Lord," the mindset makes up for the pace set by the world.

Of course, there are times when I am exhausted because of this place and its pace, but this race is worth it as I am "strengthened with all might, according to His glorious power, for all patience and longsuffering with joy" (Colossians 1:11). My eyes will again find themselves "running heavy," but as long as I can transform my mind to "walking steady," then I am able to control the pace of my confinement—a pace that is set at peace.

37. The Release That Matters Most

Life never made more sense than it does now in confinement. Physical freedom was a curse for me because of the way I used it. I misplaced my trust and misapplied my time. But now incarcerated, I would not trade the spiritual freedom and deliverance that I have today, not even for my physical release. You may call me crazy—stir-crazy—but my *View Apart* claims that I refuse to leave these walls unprepared and ill-equipped for what lies ahead. I must concentrate now on the release that matters most.

One Monday night, at the weekly service called Male Leadership, Pastor Victor Hudson changed the way I viewed confinement. He exhorted us not to be concerned with our release dates, but on the release that matters most. What negative and worldly qualities are we releasing while here? What do we need to release that is holding us back from spiritual freedom?

I am now convinced that being mentally and spiritually confined are far worse than any physical prison. No warden, prison or Department of Corrections can make me any freer than I am today. I am no longer looking ahead to a release date, but I am looking at what I have to release now that is holding me back. I claim this wholeheartedly—testifying to the truth that through Christ, I am set free, so I must stand fast in liberty and never be entangled again with a yoke of bondage (Galatians 5:1, paraphrased).

> ## Holding onto the old will keep one from the new.

I pray daily that God would continue to show me the old sinful qualities that I must release to be new. What else do I have to strip away by the Refiner's fire in this *prison purifying process*? I know all too well that we can become blind to our own faults (or blemishes), and usually any attempts by others to correct (or shape) us are unwelcomed.

Many of my peers resist the reshaping process and remain focused on that release date far ahead. Eventually that 'focal point' comes clearly into view, but they leave in the same unshaped and unformed condition as they appeared when they entered. Many of them long for the wrong release—they fail to recognize that the process of prison is God's method of working out the imperfections in our character. Without this reshaping, reforming, and releasing being done, we remain the same vessels of old: unusable, unattractive, and unrefined. We must let go!

"But now, O Lord, You are our Father; we are the clay, and You our potter; and all we are the work of Your hand" (Isaiah 64:8).

The release that matters most in confinement: Let go and let God work it out. Had I continued to look ahead to my physical release date, I never would have found my spiritual release—the day I welcomed He who sits as refiner and purifier (Malachi 3:3). There is more for me to release, and I am in the right hands for the forming and on the right pottery wheel for the shaping. Physical freedom was once a curse for me, and I am thankful that He took my curse and set me free. Life never made more sense than it does now—*Imprisoned by Peace.*

38. Circus Acts

I often wonder as I sit in my area prior to writing down my thoughts, how many times can I honestly analyze my environment without beating the same animal over and over again. Then I realize this place is a circus; and just as a child never gets tired of a circus act, I too am intrigued by human behavior. Thankfully, there are new and insightful lessons to learn in every situation.

There is always a human tendency, behavior or response to ponder upon—for instance, why does an inmate drag his chair instead of picking it up? Why do some turn up the volume on their radios and their voice boxes when lights go out at bedtime and sleep is the desired state for others? Surely there is a rational explanation for these behaviors. WRONG!

Just as the circus animal has no apprehension of the audience's appreciation, the selfish inmate is oblivious to his annoying performance. Dragging a chair along a concrete floor produces a loud noise that is obnoxious and offensive—such an act is careless at best. Blasting music at night or yelling down the tier while everyone is trying to sleep is absurdly unnecessary—such an act is senseless at best.

What would compel a person to carry out these acts? Is anyone else aware of these circus acts being performed or am I the sole beneficiary of these "entertainments"? I need to solve this puzzle! So, no longer in the amused stage, I transition my mind to the *muse* stage (a state of deep thought) to better understand why "we do what we do"! The first, most natural and obvious conclusion: The offenders are visually or hearing impaired. Yet, observation reveals that they can clearly see and hear—so that is not the problem.

However, deeper examination of the evidence suddenly discloses the logical and reasonable answer. When we can be that excessively selfish, our vision becomes a menace to true sight and our hearing a menace to true listening. When we believe we are the center stage and our selfish attitude rules, those around us will always lose. Egocentrism blinds the eyes and deafens the ears for that individual only sees what is good for *him* and only hears what is good for *him*. These external capabilities become disabilities because of the preoccupation with one's own internal world.

My *View Apart* perceives that visual and auditory acuity begin inwardly. When discord exists within, that conflict will ultimately come out, suffocating our faculties.

> **Tension ceases to exist in a man when he is able to remove "self" as the motivator in his actions.**

Then and only then will we see and hear outwardly with the proper perception. I contemplate such thoughts to learn and grow, and had I not watched carefully the circus acts around, I would have missed the reason for the show. On to the next performance.

39. Paper Value

Paper holds a whole new worth to an individual who is in prison. The majority of inmates do not receive a newspaper in the mail because one must have people on the outside to set up the process. Hence, those newspapers that do make it in to the inmates are circulated throughout the general population—passed from person to person long after the news printed on the paper is considered newsworthy. Eventually, the untimely information is irrelevant, and the end result is always the same as the newspaper ends up in the recycling bin. This holds true on the streets as well, where old newspapers may be used to wrap dead fish. Despite the consistently changing nature of news, the newspapers remain a popular item and each edition is heavily sought after by the inmates.

And then we have the other greatly coveted paper in prison. This paper is so prized it is more widely stolen than any other paper in the prison, even though this paper ultimately ends up flushed down the toilet bowl. I have witnessed fights over missing toilet paper, and I have learned this is paper that is not meant to be shared. Toilet paper never seemed so precious, and unfortunately there are no reserves in a nearby closet nor can there be a quick trip to the store for more TP. Inmates are provided approximately two rolls per month, which—for the next four weeks or so—must serve as their toilet paper, napkins, paper towels, facial tissues, and whatever other paper used to wipe up or wipe down. This thin, flimsy, almost transparent paper plays a critical role in cleanliness. It is the most cherished paper behind bars, but it still ends up worthless and discarded—not even capable of being recycled. This holds true on the streets as well.

Then there is the abundance of literature found in prison. Printed works of all sorts: from magazines to novels; fiction or nonfiction; and every conceivable genre. Most inmates enjoy a good book; and these items are passed down, passed around, donated, and shared. The value of the magazines and books depends on the preferences of the inmates. A favorite pick for most inmates are "flick" books. Flick books are pornography, and inmates have no shame in the darker uses of this type of paper.

Which brings me to the observation that has prompted this contemplation and how the value of paper is always credited to what is printed on it or what purpose it serves. I have observed that the majority of inmates, regardless of their religious standing or affiliation, treat this one book with a certain regard: THE HOLY BIBLE.

They may not believe it. They may verbally discredit it or abuse it, but they dare not throw that book away. As with the American flag, most esteem the Bible and show respect and deference in its treatment. I find this intriguing and conclude that the printed paper within the Bible has value. Even if an inmate does not personally ascribe to the words printed inside, he still recognizes that those words have worth—because of the impact they have on others. Paper in prison is valuable, depending on its impact.

"My son, keep my words, and treasure my commands within you. Keep my commands and live, and my law as the apple of your eye. Bind them on your fingers; WRITE THEM ON THE TABLET OF YOUR HEART" (Proverbs 7:1-3, emphasis mine).

> **The point of this *View Apart* is that if paper takes on such significant value when the Word of God is printed on it, how much more value do we take on if the Word is written on our hearts!**

Many value the Bible, but we must allow the Word to bring value to us. What paper do you value?

40. Passing Time in Beauty

Many people would like to know how time is spent in prison. I would rearrange this inquiry and reply: "Prison is spent on how one views the time." It is really simple when we are able to see things from the right perspective. I cannot claim to always have the right view, but I am only able to report or respond to the original question about prison from a *View Apart*: a view that is by faith and not by sight, and a view that comes from being *Imprisoned by Peace*.

It is a common precept to say that all things will eventually pass, except God's word, but what is done with the time that passes? The difference between the time spent in prison and how a prisoner spends his time is the difference between ugliness and beauty. An inmate passes his time in ugliness when he chooses the wrong things as time passes. Likewise, an inmate passes his time in beauty when he chooses the right things as time passes. When we spend time with either attribute, we begin to take on its appearance.

"What profit has the worker from that in which he labors? I have seen the God-given task with which the sons of men are

to be occupied. He has made everything beautiful in its time"
(Ecclesiastes 3:9-11).

In its time. Time spent wrapped up in ourselves will eventually come unraveled at the seams. Time spent filling our minds with toxic material will eventually spew out like vomit. The way we spend our time will eventually display its beauty or its ugliness in our lives. Thus, how time is spent in prison ultimately makes or breaks our future appearance upon release. "He has made everything beautiful in its time."

In its time. Time spent selfless at heart will eventually show less of oneself and more of the One (Christ) who lives in my heart.

> **Time spent using my pain as passion will eventually help others with their pain, which passes eventually.**

Time spent filling my mind with God's Word will eventually flow outward like rivers of life. This time will eventually pass, but how I spend it will last eternally. I spend this time working on the ugly in my character by using the beauty of Jesus to polish me, inside out. Christ isn't finished with me yet, but I am confident that He who has begun a good work in me will complete it (Philippians 1:6).

In its time. All things eventually pass, but how I use the time that passes matters most on how I view the passing time. I see freedom in this time. I see character sharpening. I see peace through confinement. I see restoration after repentance because God gives beauty (restoration) for ashes (grief and repentance) (Isaiah 61:3, paraphrased).

Even as I have spent time writing these contemplations, I see the time that has passed as purpose-filled and Lord-willed. In spite of the ugliness around me—the cursing, the lust, the evil, the hate, the envy—I see outwardly what I have committed inwardly. "[W]hile we do not look at the things which are seen, but at the things which are not seen. For the things which are seen are temporary, but the things which are not seen are eternal" (II Corinthians 4:18).

How do you view your time? What are you attracted to as time passes? This too shall pass, all things eventually do, even these 40 contemplations. Perhaps as you are reading these messages, my time spent in prison will have passed; but whether I am here or there, I am passing time in beauty!

About the Author

Matthew Maher is a 2007 graduate of Temple University, where he earned his Bachelor of Science degree in Business Administration with a concentration in Legal Studies. He is also a former professional soccer player, playing on teams in North Carolina, New Jersey, and Philadelphia respectively.

In addition, he is the President of *Soldiers for Faith Ministries (www.SoldiersForFaith.com)*, as well as the Director of Student Ministries at Coastal Christian Ocean City, where his mission is to instigate integrity, inspire conscience, and influence conduct in Christ. His "Decisions Determine Destiny" assemblies are sponsored by State Farm and service youth in his home state of New Jersey. Likewise, as an independent speaker, he also delivers uniquely catered messages wherever requested, nationally or locally.

Matthew's journey is a cautionary tale of success and failure, redemption and forgiveness. His story previously entitled, "I'm That Guy" has been presented to high schools and colleges around the country. His once admirable life was derailed by a subsequent bad decision that landed him in N.J. State prison where he served four years and seven months, and was released August 2014. You can learn more atwww.themattmaherstory.com, where his blogs have been read by over 500,000 people in every state, 121 countries, and in 67 different languages.

Matthew and his beautiful wife, Sarah, reside in Ocean City, NJ. Follow him on Twitter @mattmaherstory and on Instagram @matthewmaher7.

Other book(s) by the Author: *U MAY B THE ONLY BIBLE SOMEBODY READS: R U LEGIBLE?*

PUBLISHING

IF YOU ENJOYED THIS BOOK, WILL YOU CONSIDER SHARING THE INFLUENCE WITH OTHERS?

- Mention the book in a Facebook post, Twitter update, Pinterest pin, blog post, or Instagram pic.
- Recommend this book to those in your small group, book club, Bible study, workplace, and classes.
- Go to www.facebook.com/MatthewJMaher, "FOLLOW" and write a review or post a comment as to what you enjoyed the most.
- Tweet "I recommend reading #ImprisonedByPeace by @mattmaherstory // @5511publishing."
- Pick up a copy for someone you know who would be spiritually challenged and biblically charged by this message.
- Write a review on amazon.com, bn.com, goodreads.com, or cbd.com

FOR MORE LITERARY INFLUENCE PLEASE VISIT US AT
www.5511publishing.com

FOLLOW THE AUTHOR ON TWITTER
@mattmaherstory

FOLLOW THE AUTHOR ON INSTAGRAM
@matthewmaher7

About THE CORE CONVICTION SERIES

You have just read Book #1 of the *Core Convictions Series.* Please be on the look out for additional books in this series, as each unique publication looks to embolden the believer's conviction in Christ.

Matthew Maher says, *"I'd rather stand alone with Jesus than sit in a crowd without Him."*